D1031367

Praying Through Scripture
A Woman's Journal

KIM MELNICK

Prayer Journal Press

Praying Through Scripture - A Woman's Journal
© 2017 by Kim Melnick
Prayer Journal Press
ISBN 978-0-9995857-0-2 (e-Book version)
ISBN 978-0-9995857-1-9 (paperback version)

All rights reserved. No part of this book may be reproduced or utilized in any form or by any means, electronic or mechanical, or by any information storage and retrieval system - except for brief quotations for the purpose of review, without written permission from the author or publisher.

All inquiries should be sent through Contact page on our website, www.PrayWithScripture.com.

All Scripture quotations, unless otherwise indicated, are taken from the Holy Bible, New International Version®, NIV®. Copyright ©1973, 1978, 1984, 2011 by Biblica, Inc.™ Used by permission of Zondervan. All rights reserved worldwide. www.zondervan.com The "NIV" and "New International Version" are trademarks registered in the United States Patent and Trademark Office by Biblica, Inc.™

Cover design and layout by Jeff Melnick, High Impact Advertising LLC (www.hiashop.com)

Page design inspired by Amanda Melnick

Printed in the United States of America

2017 - First Edition

Foreword

Prayer Warrior Wannabe

I wrote this book for myself. Seriously. While that may seem a little strange, it's the truth.

I have loved Jesus for many years. I love His Word and I'm pretty faithful in reading or studying it everyday. I love to listen to sermons and be wowed by some mind-blowing connection between the Old and New Testaments that I had missed. I love when a familiar passage takes on new depth as I learn the true meaning of a word in the original Greek or Hebrew. In short, I LOVE learning about our amazing God through His Word.

But with prayer, I struggle. For years, I wanted to love prayer, to be that woman who rises early and often, who spends long and precious moments with the Lord in praise of Him and in supplication for others and for herself. However, I'm not that woman. When I pray early, my mind wanders to the demands of the day. When I pray late, my energy wanes and sleep overtakes me and often cannot find words to express what my heart longs to say.

Years ago, I learned the "secret of prayer" from a favorite pastor's sermon. He said to simply make GOD'S will YOUR wants. Then, ask for whatever you want! I loved this idea and sought ways to apply it to my prayer life. I began asking God, after a time of reading or studying, to show me how to use what I just learned about Him/His will to pray for myself and those around me.

This was helpful, but I still felt distracted in my prayer time. On top of that, there were people and situations that I desired to pray for on a regular basis, but still did not do so. That's where the writing of this book begins….

I began collecting verses and organizing them by categories of prayer - by topics that I wanted to pray for regularly. Initially, there were verses scribbled on various pieces of notebook paper and in prayer journals. Eventually, they were organized. As I began to use them in my personal prayer time, I learned that these categories really did help my focus. And, by praying specific bible verses with each category, I no longer had to "find" the words to pray. God had already given them to me.

With much help from my husband (and some design input from my 12 year old), this book began to take shape. Instead of normal "proof-reading," this book was checked through "prayer-reading." I've prayed through every verse and every page and asked some friends to do the same.

While I'm still a Prayer Warrior Wannabe, thanks to the grace of God and the contents of this book, I've come a long way!

How to Use This Book

I'm sure there are countless ways to use this book, but here I will cover how I use it. Each "section" of the book is six pages long and I recommend using a section for one to two weeks.

Categories/Topics (Listed at the top of each column)
The first page of each section is designed to prepare your heart and mind to pray: Adoration, Confession and Thanksgiving. These are pretty self-explanatory and the verses given for Adoration and Thanksgiving make it easy to give praise and thanks to the Lord.

With Confession, there is also a verse to pray, reminding us of our sinful nature and of God's grace and mercy in forgiveness. When I'm reflecting on my own sin, I often examine my past day/week while reflecting on the fruits of the Spirit (love, joy, patience, kindness, goodness, faithfulness). This allows me to quickly identify sin in my life.

The remaining categories are listed below along with prompts on how I view this category....

Children - My own children/others I know or care about

Marriages - My marriage, married friends, marriages in my church, engaged couples, my own children whom I hope to see find a Godly spouse

Finances/Stewardship - My own/those around me, especially those who are struggling

The Church - The body of Christ where I worship and the Church worldwide

Nation/Leaders - Our President, Congress and other national/state/local leaders and citizens

Missionaries - Those who have left home to share the Gospel of Jesus full-time

The Lost - Family/Friends/Acquaintances whose lives have not been transformed by the Gospel of Jesus Christ

The Sick, Weary & Discouraged - General category for those burdened by various struggles

The Oppressed & Enslaved - General category that might include those who are suffering from persecution, addiction, or caught human trafficking

Wisdom - For myself and those who are in situations where a need for wisdom is apparent

Daily Walk - Myself and others who may be struggling with faithfulness, obedience, etc

Gratitude & Joy - Myself and others who need a reminder that we always have a reason for joy and gratitude

How to Use This Book

Bible Verses
I encourage you to read the verse a few times. Consider how you might pray this verse for the people or situations that come to mind with the prompt. In most instances, I actually pray the verse back to God. For example, if I'm praying Proverbs 5:16 for my husband, I might say, "Lord, help Jeff to shine your light today that others may see his good deeds and glorify you."

Journal Space
Some of you love to journal; others hate it. This space was intentionally left small for those who might be intimidated by large chunks of lined space. If you love to write out long prayers, go for it and know that there is full page of journaling at the end of each week's section if you run out of room. I personally love the idea of journaling more than the actual practice of journaling out long passages or prayers, so I use the space to make lists or bullet points. I would encourage you to write something, even if it's just a few words. It will help keep you focused, and you will have a resource to look back and see how God worked in various situations.

Weird Letters at the Bottom of the Page
Those weird letters at the bottom of the page are not typos. They are a tool to help you memorize Scripture. Each letter is the first letter of every word in the verses listed on the page. You can look at the letters and recall the words pretty easily. If you do this regularly, you will have memorized the verse. If you make this a practice as you pray, this book will help you memorize sixty verses as you pray.

Adoration

He says, "Be still, and know that I am God;
I will be exalted among the nations,
I will be exalted in the earth."
Psalm 46:10

- Quiet
- Pigeons floating through air

Confession

If we confess our sins, he is faithful and just and
will forgive us our sins and purify us from all
unrighteousness.
1 John 1: 9

Thanksgiving

Give thanks to the Lord, for he is good;
his love endures forever.
1 Chronicles 16:34

H S, "B S, A K T I A G; I W B E A T N, I W B E I T E." - Psalm 46:10

I W C O S, H I F A J A W F U O S A P U F A U. - 1 John 1:9

G T T T L, F H I G; H L E F. - 1 Chronicles 16:34

Children

And Jesus grew in wisdom and stature,
and in favor with God and man.
Luke 2:52

Marriages

By wisdom a house is built,
and through understanding it is established;
Through knowledge its rooms are filled
with rare and beautiful treasures.
Proverbs 24:3-4

Finances & Stewardship

And my God will meet all your needs
according to the riches of his glory
in Christ Jesus.
Philippians 4:19

A J G I W A S, A I F W G A M. - Luke 2:52

B W A H I B, A T U I I E; T K I R A F W R A B T. - Proverbs 24:3-4

A M G W M A Y N A T T R O H G I C J. - Philippians 4:19

The Church

Be devoted to one another in love. Honor
one another above yourselves. Never be
lacking in zeal, but keep your spiritual
fervor, serving the Lord. Be joyful in hope,
patient in affliction, faithful in prayer.
Share with the Lord's people who are in need.
Practice hospitality.
Romans 12: 10-13

Nations & Leaders

Let everyone be subject to the governing
authorities, for there is no authority
except that which God has established.
The authorities that exist have been
established by God.
Romans 13:1

Missionaries

As for other matters, brothers and sisters,
pray for us that the message of the Lord
may spread rapidly and be honored, just
as it was with you.
2 Thessalonians 3:1

B D T O A I L. H O A A Y. N B L I Z, B K Y S F, S T L. B J I H, P I A, F I P. S W T L P W A I N. P H. - Romans 12:10-13

L E B S T T G A, F T I N A E T W G H E. T A T E H B E B G. - Romans 13:1

A F O M, B A S, P F U T T M O T L M S R A B H, J A I W W Y. - 2 Thessalonians 3:1

The Lost

For the Son of Man came to seek
and to save the lost.
Luke 19:10

The Sick, Weary
& Discouraged

The Lord is close to the brokenhearted
and saves those who are crushed in spirit.
Psalm 34:18

The Oppressed
& Enslaved

The Lord is a refuge for the oppressed, a
stronghold in times of trouble. Those who
know your name trust in you, for you, Lord,
have never forsaken those who seek you.
Psalm 7:9-10

FTSOMCTSATSTL. - Luke 19:10

TLICTTBASTWACIS. - Psalm 34:18

TLIARFTO, ASITOT. TWKYNTIY, FY, L, HNFTWSY. - Psalm 7:9-10

Wisdom

If any of you lacks wisdom, you should ask God, who gives generously to all without finding fault, and it will be given to you.
James 1:5

Daily Walk

Therefore, I urge you, brothers and sisters, in view of God's mercy, to offer your bodies as a living sacrifice, holy and pleasing to God - this is your true and proper worship. Do not conform to the pattern of this world, but be transformed by the renewing of your mind. Then you will be able to test and approve what God's will is - his good, pleasing andperfect will.
Romans 12:1-2

Gratitude & Joy

Rejoice always, pray continually, give thanks in all circumstances; for this is God's will for you in Christ Jesus.
1 Thessalonians 5:16-18

I A O Y L W, Y S A G, W G G T A W F F, A I W B G T Y. - James 1:5

T, I R Y, B A S, I V O G M, T O Y B A A L S, H A P T G - T I Y T A P W. D N C T T P O T W, B B T B T R O Y M. T Y W B A T T A A W G W I - H G, P A P W. - Romans 12:1-2

R A, P C, G T I A C; F T I G W F Y I C J. - 1 Thessalonians 5:16-18

Adoration

The heavens declare the glory of God; the
skies proclaim the work of his hands.
Day after day they pour forth speech; night
after night they reveal knowledge.
Psalm 19:1-2

Confession

...for all have sinned and fall short of the glory
of God, and all are justified freely by his
grace through the redemption that
came by Christ Jesus.
Romans 3:23-24

Thanksgiving

I will give thanks to you, Lord, with all my
heart; I will tell of all your wonderful deeds.
I will be glad and rejoice in you; I will sing
the praises of your name, O Most High.
Psalm 9:1-2

THDTGOG, TSPTWOHH. DADTPFS; NANTRK. - Psalm 19:1-2

FAHSAFSOTGOG, AAAJFBHGTTRTCBC J. - Romans 3:23-24

IWGTTY, L, WAMH; IWTOAYWD. IWBGARIY; IWSTPOYN, OMH. - Psalm 9:1-2

Children

…so that Christ may dwell in your hearts through faith. And I pray that you, being rooted and established in love, may have power, together with all the Lord's holy people, to grasp how wide and long and high and deep is the love of Christ.
Ephesians 3:17-18

Marriages

Above all, love each other deeply, because love covers over a multitude of sins.
1 Peter 4:8

Finances & Stewardship

So do not worry, saying, 'What shall we eat?' or 'What shall we drink?' or 'What shall we wear?' For the pagans run after all these things, and your heavenly Father knows that you need them. But seek first his kingdom and his righteousness, and all these things will be given to you as well.
Matthew 6: 31-33

…S T C M D I Y H T F. A I P T Y, B R A E I L, M H P, T W A T L H P, T G H W A L A H A D I T L O C. - Ephesians 3:17-18

A A, L E O D, B L C O A M O S. - 1 Peter 4:8

S D N W, S, 'W S W E?' or 'W S W D?' or 'W S W W?' F T P R A A T T, A Y H F K T Y N T. B S F H K A H R, A A T T W B G T Y A W. - Matthew 6:31-33

The Church

Bless those who persecute you; bless and do not curse. Rejoice with those who rejoice; mourn with those who mourn. Live in harmony with one another. Do not be proud, but be willing to associate with people of low position. Do not be conceited.
Romans 12:14-16

Nations & Leaders

Show proper respect to everyone, love the family of believers, fear God, honor the emperor.
1 Peter 2:17

Missionaries

Declare his glory among the nations, his marvelous deeds among all peoples.
Psalm 96:3

BTWPY; BADNC. RWTWR; MWTWM. LIHWOA.
DNBP, BBWTAWPOLP. DNBC. - Romans 12:14-16

SPRTE, LTFOB, FG, HTE. - 1 Peter 2:17

DHGATN, HMDAAP. - Psalm 96:3

The Lost

The Lord is not slow in keeping his promise, as some understand slowness. Instead he is patient with you, not wanting anyone to perish, but everyone to come to repentance.
2 Peter 3:9

The Sick, Weary & Discouraged

We are hard pressed on every side, but not crushed; perplexed, but not in despair; persecuted, but not abandoned; struck down, but not destroyed.
2 Corinthians 4:8-9

The Oppressed & Enslaved

He defends the cause of the fatherless and the widow, and loves the foreigner residing among you, giving them food and clothing.
Deuteronomy 10:18

TLINSIKHP, ASUS. IHIPWY, NWATP, BETCTR. - 2 Peter 3:9

WAHPOES, BNC; P, BNID; P, BNA; SD, BND. - 2 Corinthians 4:8-9

HDTCOTFATW, ALTFRAY, GTFAC. - Deuteronomy 10:18

Wisdom

But the wisdom that comes from heaven is first of all pure; then peace-loving, considerate, submissive, full of mercy and good fruit, impartial and sincere.
James 3:17

Daily Walk

He answered, "Love the Lord your God with all your heart and with all your soul and with all your strength and with all your mind" and, "Love your neighbor as yourself."
Luke 10:27

Gratitude & Joy

I will give thanks to you, Lord, with all my heart; I will tell of all your wonderful deeds. I will be glad and rejoice in you; I will sing the praises of your name, O Most High.
Psalm 9:1-2

BTWTCFHIFOAP; TP-L, C, S, FOMAGF, I A S. - James 3:17

HA, "LTLYGWALYHAWAYSAWAYSAWAYM" A, "LYNAY." - Luke 10:27

IWGTTY, L, WAMH; IWTOAYWD. IWBGARIY; IWSTPOYN, OMH. - Psalm 9:1-2

Adoration

Because your love is better than life, my lips will glorify you. I will praise you as long as I live, and in your name I will lift up my hands. I will be fully satisfied as with the richest of foods; with singing lips my mouth will praise you.
Psalm 63: 3-5

Confession

Whoever conceals their sins does not prosper, but the one who confesses and renounces them finds mercy.
Proverbs 28:13

Thanksgiving

Rejoice always, pray continually, give thanks in all circumstances; for this is God's will for you in Christ Jesus.
1 Thessalonians 5:16-18

B Y L I B T L, M L W G Y. I W P Y A L A I L, A I Y N I W L U M H. I W
B F S A W T R O F; W S L M M W P Y. - Psalm 63:3-5

W C T S D N P, B T O W C A R T F M. - Proverbs 28:13

R A, P C, G T I A C; F T I G W F Y I C J. - 1 Thessalonians 5:16-18

Children

Trust in the Lord with all your heart
and lean not on your own understanding;
in all your ways submit to him,
and he will make your paths straight.
Proverbs 3:5-6

Marriages

Be kind and compassionate to one
another, forgiving each other,
just as in Christ God forgave you.
Ephesians 4:32

Finances & Stewardship

Do not store up for yourselves treasures on
earth, where moths and vermin destroy,
and where thieves break in and steal.
But store up for yourselves treasures in
heaven, where moths and vermin do
not destroy, and where thieves do not
break in and steal. For where your treasure
is, there your heart will be also.
Matthew 6:19-21

TITLWAYHALNOYOU; IAYWSTH, AHWMYPS. - Proverbs 3:5-6

BKACTOA, FEO, JAICGFY. - Ephesians 4:32

DNSUFYTOE, WMAVD, AWTBIAS. BSUFYTIH,
WMAVDND, AWTDNBIAS. FWYTI, TYHWBA. Matthew 6:19-21

The Church

Devote yourselves to prayer, being watchful
and thankful. And pray for us, too, that
God may open a door for our message, so
that we may proclaim the mystery of
Christ, for which I am in chains.
Colossians 4:2-3

Nations & Leaders

I urge, then, first of all, that petitions, prayers,
intercession and thanksgiving be made for all
people— for kings and all those in authority,
that we may live peaceful and quiet lives
in all godliness and holiness.
1 Timothy 2:1-2

Missionaries

Pray also for me, that whenever I speak,
words may be given me so that I will
fearlessly make known the mystery
of the gospel…
Ephesians 3:19

D Y T P, B W A T. A P F U, T, T G M O A D F O M, S T W M P T M O C, F W I A I C. - Colossians 4:2-3

I U, T, F O A, T P, P, I A T B M F A P - F K A A T I A, T W M L P A Q L I A G A H. - 1 Timothy 2:1-2

P A F M, T W I S, W M B G M S T I W F M K T M O T G… - Ephesians 3:19

The Lost

For God so loved the world that he
gave his one and only Son,
that whoever believes in him shall not
perish but have eternal life.
John 3:16

The Sick, Weary & Discouraged

He heals the brokenhearted and
bandages their wounds.
Psalm 147:3

The Oppressed & Enslaved

The Lord sets prisoners free, the Lord gives
sight to the blind, the Lord lifts up those
who are bowed down, the Lord loves the
righteous. The Lord watches over the
foreigner and sustains the fatherless and
the widow, but he frustrates the
ways of the wicked.
Psalm 146:7-9

F G S L T W T H G H O A O S, T W B I H S N P B H E L. - John 3:16

H H T B A B T W. - Psalm 147:3

T L S P F, T L G S T T B, T L L U T W A B D, T L L T R.
T L W O T F A S T F A T W, B H F T W O T W. - Psalm 146:7-9

Wisdom

The fear of the Lord is the beginning of
knowledge, but fools despise
wisdom and instruction.
Proverbs 1:7

Daily Walk

In the same way, let your light shine
before others, that they may
see your good deeds and
glorify your Father in heaven.
Matthew 5:16

Gratitude &
Joy

Give thanks to the Lord, for he is good; his
love endures forever. Let the redeemed of
the Lord tell their story—those he
redeemed from the hand of the foe…
Psalm 107:1-2

T F O T L I T B O K, B F D W A I. - Proverbs 1:7

I T S W, L Y L S B O, T T M S Y G D A G Y F I H. - Matthew 5:16

G T T T L, F H I G; H L E F. L T R O T L T T S - T H R F T H O T F… - Psalm 107:1-2

Adoration

It is good to praise the Lord and make
music to your name, O Most High,
proclaiming your love in the morning
and your faithfulness at night...
Psalm 92:1-2

Confession

Therefore confess your sins to each other
and pray for each other so that you may be
healed. The prayer of a righteous person is
powerful and effective.
James 5:16

Thanksgiving

So then, just as you received Christ Jesus
as Lord, continue to live your lives in him,
rooted and built up in him, strengthened
in the faith as you were taught, and
overflowing with thankfulness.
Colossians 2:6-7

I I G T P T L A M M T Y N, O M H, P Y L I T M A Y F A N... - Psalm 92:1-2

T C Y S T E O A P F E O S T Y M B H. T P O A R P I P A E. - James 5:16

S T, J A Y R C J A L, C T L Y L I H, R A B U I H, S I T F A Y W T, A O W T. - Colossians 2:6-7

Children

But grow in the grace and knowledge
of our Lord and Savior Jesus Christ.
To him be glory both now
and forever! Amen.
2 Peter 3:18

Marriages

Submit to one another out of
reverence for Christ.
Ephesians 5:21

Finances & Stewardship

I know what it is to be in need, and I know
what it is to have plenty. I have learned
the secret of being content in any and
every situation, whether well fed or
hungry, whether living in plenty or in
want. I can do all this through him
who gives me strength.
Philippians 4:12-13

B G I T G A K O O L A S J C. T H B G B N A F! A. - 2 Peter 3:18

S T O A O O R F C. - Ephesians 5:21

I K W I I T B I N, A I K W I I T H P. I H L T S O B C I A A E S, W W F O H,
W L I P O I W. I C D A T T H W G M S. - PHILIPPIANS 4:12-13

The Church

As a prisoner for the Lord, then, I urge you
to live a life worthy of the calling you have
received. Be completely humble and gentle;
be patient, bearing with one another in love.
Make every effort to keep the unity of
the Spirit through the bond of peace.
Ephesians 4:1-3

Nations & Leaders

For lack of guidance a nation falls,
but victory is won through
many advisers.
Proverbs 11:14

Missionaries

Therefore go and make disciples of all nations,
baptizing them in the name of the Father
and of the Son and of the Holy Spirit, and
teaching them to obey everything I have
commanded you. And surely I am with
you always, to the very end of the age."
Matthew 28:19-20

A A P F T L, T, I U Y T L A L W O T C Y H R. B C H A G; B P, B W O A I L.
M E E T K T U O T S T T B O P. - Ephesians 4:1-3

F L O G A N F, B V I W T M A. - Proverbs 11:14

T G A M D O A N, B T I T N O T F A O T S A O T H S, A T T
T O E I H C Y. A S I A W Y A, T T V E O T A." - Mathew 28:19-20

The Lost

For God did not send his Son into the world to condemn the world, but to save the world through him.
John 3:17

The Sick, Weary & Discouraged

God is our refuge and strength, an ever-present help in trouble. Therefore we will not fear, though the earth give way and the mountains fall into the heart of the sea, though its waters roar and foam and the mountains quake with their surging.
Psalm 46:1-3

The Oppressed & Enslaved

This is what the Lord Almighty said: "Administer true justice; show mercy and compassion to one another. Do not oppress the widow or the fatherless, the foreigner or the poor. Do not plot evil against each other.'"
Zechariah 7:9-10

F G D N S H S I T W T C T W, B T S T W T H. - John 3:17

G I O R A S, A E H I T. T W W N F, T T E G W A T M F I T H O T S, T I W R A F A T M Q W T S. - Psalm 46:1-3

T I W T L A S: "A T J; S M A C T O A. D N O T W O T F, T F O T P. D N P E A E O." - Zechariah 7:9-10

Wisdom

My goal is that they may be encouraged in heart and united in love, so that they may have the full riches of complete understanding, in order that they may know the mystery of God, namely, Christ, in whom are hidden all the treasures of wisdom and knowledge.
Colossians 2:2-3

Daily Walk

So whether you eat or drink or whatever you do, do it all for the glory of God.
1 Corinthians 10:31

Gratitude & Joy

Therefore, since we are receiving a kingdom that cannot be shaken, let us be thankful, and so worship God acceptably with reverence and awe, for our "God is a consuming fire."
Hebrews 12:28-29

MGITTMBEIHAUIL, STTMHTFROCU, IOTTM KTMOG, N, C, IWAHATTOWAK. - Colossians 2:2-3

SWYEODOWYD, DIAFTGOG. - 1 Corinthians 10:31

T, SWARAKTCBS, LUBT, ASWGAWRAA, FO "GIACF." - Hebrews 12:28-29

Adoration

He says, "Be still, and know that I am God;
I will be exalted among the nations,
I will be exalted in the earth."
Psalm 46:10

Confession

If we confess our sins, he is faithful and just and
will forgive us our sins and purify us from all
unrighteousness.
1 John 1: 9

Thanksgiving

Give thanks to the Lord, for he is good;
his love endures forever.
1 Chronicles 16:34

H S, "B S, A K T I A G; I W B E A T N, I W B E I T E." - Psalm 46:10

I W C O S, H I F A J A W F U O S A P U F A U. - 1 John 1:9

G T T T L, F H I G; H L E F. - 1 Chronicles 16:34

Children

And Jesus grew in wisdom and stature,
and in favor with God and man.
Luke 2:52

Marriages

By wisdom a house is built,
and through understanding it is established;
Through knowledge its rooms are filled
with rare and beautiful treasures.
Proverbs 24:3-4

Finances & Stewardship

And my God will meet all your needs
according to the riches of his glory
in Christ Jesus.
Philippians 4:19

A J G I W A S, A I F W G A M. - Luke 2:52

B W A H I B, A T U I I E; T K I R A F W R A B T. - Proverbs 24:3-4

A M G W M A Y N A T T R O H G I C J. - Philippians 4:19

The Church

Be devoted to one another in love. Honor one another above yourselves. Never be lacking in zeal, but keep your spiritual fervor, serving the Lord. Be joyful in hope, patient in affliction, faithful in prayer. Share with the Lord's people who are in need. Practice hospitality.

Romans 12: 10-13

Nations & Leaders

Let everyone be subject to the governing authorities, for there is no authority except that which God has established. The authorities that exist have been established by God.

Romans 13:1

Missionaries

As for other matters, brothers and sisters, pray for us that the message of the Lord may spread rapidly and be honored, just as it was with you.

2 Thessalonians 3:1

BDTOAIL. HOAAY. NBLIZ, BKYSF, STL. BJIH, PIA, FIP. SWTLPWAIN. P H. - Romans 12:10-13

LEBSTTGA, FTINAETWGHE. TATEHBEBG. - Romans 13:1

AFOM, BAS, PFUTTMOTLMSRABH, JAIWWY. - 2 Thessalonians 3:1

The Lost

For the Son of Man came to seek
and to save the lost.
Luke 19:10

The Sick, Weary
& Discouraged

The Lord is close to the brokenhearted
and saves those who are crushed in spirit.
Psalm 34:18

The Oppressed
& Enslaved

The Lord is a refuge for the oppressed, a
stronghold in times of trouble. Those who
know your name trust in you, for you, Lord,
have never forsaken those who seek you.
Psalm 7:9-10

FTSOMCTSATSTL. - Luke 19:10

TLICTTBASTWACIS. - Psalm 34:18

TLIARFTO, ASITOT. TWKYNTIY, FY, L, HNFTWSY. - Psalm 7:9-10

Wisdom

If any of you lacks wisdom, you should ask God, who gives generously to all without finding fault, and it will be given to you.
James 1:5

Daily Walk

Therefore, I urge you, brothers and sisters, in view of God's mercy, to offer your bodies as a living sacrifice, holy and pleasing to God - this is your true and proper worship. Do not conform to the pattern of this world, but be transformed by the renewing of your mind. Then you will be able to test and approve what God's will is - his good, pleasing andperfect will.
Romans 12:1-2

Gratitude & Joy

Rejoice always, pray continually, give thanks in all circumstances; for this is God's will for you in Christ Jesus.
1 Thessalonians 5:16-18

I A O Y L W, Y S A G, W G G T A W F F, A I W B G T Y. - James 1:5

T, I R Y, B A S, I V O G M, T O Y B A A L S, H A P T G - T I Y T A P W. D N C T T P O T W,
B B T B T R O Y M. T Y W B A T T A A W G W I - H G, P A P W. - Romans 12:1-2

R A, P C, G T I A C; F T I G W F Y I C J. - 1 Thessalonians 5:16-18

Adoration

The heavens declare the glory of God; the
skies proclaim the work of his hands.
Day after day they pour forth speech; night
after night they reveal knowledge.
Psalm 19:1-2

Confession

…for all have sinned and fall short of the glory
of God, and all are justified freely by his
grace through the redemption that
came by Christ Jesus.
Romans 3:23-24

Thanksgiving

I will give thanks to you, Lord, with all my
heart; I will tell of all your wonderful deeds.
I will be glad and rejoice in you; I will sing
the praises of your name, O Most High.
Psalm 9:1-2

T H D T G O G, T S P T W O H H. D A D T P F S; N A N T R K. - Psalm 19:1-2

F A H S A F S O T G O G, A A A J F B H G T T R T C B C J. - Romans 3:23-24

I W G T T Y, L, W A M H; I W T O A Y W D. I W B G A R I Y; I W S T P O Y N, O M H. - Psalm 9:1-2

Children

...so that Christ may dwell in your hearts through faith. And I pray that you, being rooted and established in love, may have power, together with all the Lord's holy people, to grasp how wide and long and high and deep is the love of Christ.
Ephesians 3:17-18

Marriages

Above all, love each other deeply, because love covers over a multitude of sins.
1 Peter 4:8

Finances & Stewardship

So do not worry, saying, 'What shall we eat?' or 'What shall we drink?' or 'What shall we wear?' For the pagans run after all these things, and your heavenly Father knows that you need them. But seek first his kingdom and his righteousness, and all these things will be given to you as well.
Matthew 6: 31-33

...S T C M D I Y H T F. A I P T Y, B R A E I L, M H P, T W A T L H P, T G H W A L A H A D I T L O C. - Ephesians 3:17-18

A A, L E O D, B L C O A M O S. - 1 Peter 4:8

S D N W, S, 'W S W E?' or 'W S W D?' or 'W S W W?' F T P R A A T T, A Y H F K T Y N T. B S F H K A H R, A A T T W B G T Y A W. - Matthew 6:31-33

The Church

Bless those who persecute you; bless and do not curse. Rejoice with those who rejoice; mourn with those who mourn. Live in harmony with one another. Do not be proud, but be willing to associate with people of low position. Do not be conceited.
Romans 12:14-16

Nations & Leaders

Show proper respect to everyone, love the family of believers, fear God, honor the emperor.
1 Peter 2:17

Missionaries

Declare his glory among the nations, his marvelous deeds among all peoples.
Psalm 96:3

BTWPY; BADNC. RWTWR; MWTWM. LIHWOA.
DNBP, BBWTAWPOLP. DNBC. - Romans 12:14-16

SPRTE, LTFOB, FG, HTE. - 1 Peter 2:17

DHGATN, HMDAAP. - Psalm 96:3

The Lost

The Lord is not slow in keeping his promise,
as some understand slowness. Instead he is
patient with you, not wanting anyone to
perish, but everyone to come to repentance.
2 Peter 3:9

The Sick, Weary & Discouraged

We are hard pressed on every side, but not
crushed; perplexed, but not in despair;
persecuted, but not abandoned;
struck down, but not destroyed.
2 Corinthians 4:8-9

The Oppressed & Enslaved

He defends the cause of the fatherless
and the widow, and loves the foreigner
residing among you, giving them
food and clothing.
Deuteronomy 10:18

TLINSIKHP, ASUS. IHIPWY, NWATP, BETCTR. - 2 Peter 3:9

WAHPOES, BNC; P, BNID; P, BNA; SD, BND. - 2 Corinthians 4:8-9

HDTCOTFATW, ALTFRAY, GTFAC. - Deuteronomy 10:18

Wisdom

But the wisdom that comes from heaven is first of all pure; then peace-loving, considerate, submissive, full of mercy and good fruit, impartial and sincere.
James 3:17

Daily Walk

He answered, "Love the Lord your God with all your heart and with all your soul and with all your strength and with all your mind" and, "Love your neighbor as yourself."
Luke 10:27

Gratitude & Joy

I will give thanks to you, Lord, with all my heart; I will tell of all your wonderful deeds. I will be glad and rejoice in you; I will sing the praises of your name, O Most High.
Psalm 9:1-2

B T W T C F H I F O A P; T P-L, C, S, F O M A G F, I A S. - James 3:17

H A, "L T L Y G W A L Y H A W A Y S A W A Y S A W A Y M" A, "L Y N A Y." - Luke 10:27

I W G T T Y, L, W A M H; I W T O A Y W D. I W B G A R I Y; I W S T P O Y N, O M H. - Psalm 9:1-2

Adoration

Because your love is better than life, my lips will glorify you. I will praise you as long as I live, and in your name I will lift up my hands. I will be fully satisfied as with the richest of foods; with singing lips my mouth will praise you.
Psalm 63: 3-5

Confession

Whoever conceals their sins does not prosper, but the one who confesses and renounces them finds mercy.
Proverbs 28:13

Thanksgiving

Rejoice always, pray continually, give thanks in all circumstances; for this is God's will for you in Christ Jesus.
1 Thessalonians 5:16-18

B Y L I B T L , M L W G Y. I W P Y A L A I L , A I Y N I W L U M H. I W
B F S A W T R O F ; W S L M M W P Y. - Psalm 63:3-5

W C T S D N P , B T O W C A R T F M. - Proverbs 28:13

R A , P C , G T I A C ; F T I G W F Y I C J. - 1 Thessalonians 5:16-18

Children

Trust in the Lord with all your heart
and lean not on your own understanding;
in all your ways submit to him,
and he will make your paths straight.
Proverbs 3:5-6

Marriages

Be kind and compassionate to one
another, forgiving each other,
just as in Christ God forgave you.
Ephesians 4:32

Finances & Stewardship

Do not store up for yourselves treasures on
earth, where moths and vermin destroy,
and where thieves break in and steal.
But store up for yourselves treasures in
heaven, where moths and vermin do
not destroy, and where thieves do not
break in and steal. For where your treasure
is, there your heart will be also.
Matthew 6:19-21

TITLWAYHALNOYOU; IAYWSTH, AHWMYPS. - Proverbs 3:5-6

BKACTOA, FEO, JAICGFY. - Ephesians 4:32

DNSUFYTOE, WMAVD, AWTBIAS. BSUFYTIH,
WMAVDND, AWTDNBIAS. FWYTI, TYHWBA. Matthew 6:19-21

The Church

Devote yourselves to prayer, being watchful and thankful. And pray for us, too, that God may open a door for our message, so that we may proclaim the mystery of Christ, for which I am in chains.
Colossians 4:2-3

Nations & Leaders

I urge, then, first of all, that petitions, prayers, intercession and thanksgiving be made for all people— for kings and all those in authority, that we may live peaceful and quiet lives in all godliness and holiness.
1 Timothy 2:1-2

Missionaries

Pray also for me, that whenever I speak, words may be given me so that I will fearlessly make known the mystery of the gospel…
Ephesians 3:19

DYTP, BWAT. APFU, T, TGMOADFOM, STWMPTMOC, FWIAIC. - Colossians 4:2-3

IU, T, FOA, TP, P, IATBMFAP - FKAATIA, TWMLPAQLIAGAH. - 1 Timothy 2:1-2

PAFM, TWIS, WMBGMSTIWFMKTMOTG… - Ephesians 3:19

The Lost

For God so loved the world that he
gave his one and only Son,
that whoever believes in him shall not
perish but have eternal life.
John 3:16

The Sick, Weary
& Discouraged

He heals the brokenhearted and
bandages their wounds.
Psalm 147:3

The Oppressed
& Enslaved

The Lord sets prisoners free, the Lord gives
sight to the blind, the Lord lifts up those
who are bowed down, the Lord loves the
righteous. The Lord watches over the
foreigner and sustains the fatherless and
the widow, but he frustrates the
ways of the wicked.
Psalm 146:7-9

F G S L T W T H G H O A O S, T W B I H S N P B H E L. - John 3:16

H H T B A B T W. - Psalm 147:3

T L S P F, T L G S T T B, T L L U T W A B D, T L L T R.
T L W O T F A S T F A T W, B H F T W O T W. - Psalm 146:7-9

Wisdom

The fear of the Lord is the beginning of knowledge, but fools despise wisdom and instruction.
Proverbs 1:7

Daily Walk

In the same way, let your light shine before others, that they may see your good deeds and glorify your Father in heaven.
Matthew 5:16

Gratitude & Joy

Give thanks to the Lord, for he is good; his love endures forever. Let the redeemed of the Lord tell their story—those he redeemed from the hand of the foe…
Psalm 107:1-2

TFOTLITBOK, BFDWAI. - Proverbs 1:7

ITSW, LYLSBO, TTMSYGDAGYFIH. - Matthew 5:16

GTTTL, FHIG; HLEF. LTROTLTTS - THRFTHOTF… - Psalm 107:1-2

Adoration

It is good to praise the Lord and make music to your name, O Most High, proclaiming your love in the morning and your faithfulness at night…
Psalm 92:1-2

Confession

Therefore confess your sins to each other and pray for each other so that you may be healed. The prayer of a righteous person is powerful and effective.
James 5:16

Thanksgiving

So then, just as you received Christ Jesus as Lord, continue to live your lives in him, rooted and built up in him, strengthened in the faith as you were taught, and overflowing with thankfulness.
Colossians 2:6-7

I I G T P T L A M M T Y N, O M H, P Y L I T M A Y F A N... - Psalm 92:1-2

T C Y S T E O A P F E O S T Y M B H. T P O A R P I P A E. - James 5:16

S T, J A Y R C J A L, C T L Y L I H, R A B U I H, S I T F A Y W T, A O W T. - Colossians 2:6-7

Children

But grow in the grace and knowledge
of our Lord and Savior Jesus Christ.
To him be glory both now
and forever! Amen.
2 Peter 3:18

Marriages

Submit to one another out of
reverence for Christ.
Ephesians 5:21

Finances &
Stewardship

I know what it is to be in need, and I know
what it is to have plenty. I have learned
the secret of being content in any and
every situation, whether well fed or
hungry, whether living in plenty or in
want. I can do all this through him
who gives me strength.
Philippians 4:12-13

B G I T G A K O O L A S J C. T H B G B N A F! A. - 2 Peter 3:18

S T O A O O R F C. - Ephesians 5:21

I K W I I T B I N, A I K W I I T H P. I H L T S O B C I A A E S, W W F O H,
W L I P O I W. I C D A T T H W G M S. - PHILIPPIANS 4:12-13

The Church

As a prisoner for the Lord, then, I urge you to live a life worthy of the calling you have received. Be completely humble and gentle; be patient, bearing with one another in love. Make every effort to keep the unity of the Spirit through the bond of peace.
Ephesians 4:1-3

Nations & Leaders

For lack of guidance a nation falls, but victory is won through many advisers.
Proverbs 11:14

Missionaries

Therefore go and make disciples of all nations, baptizing them in the name of the Father and of the Son and of the Holy Spirit, and teaching them to obey everything I have commanded you. And surely I am with you always, to the very end of the age."
Matthew 28:19-20

A A P F T L, T, I U Y T L A L W O T C Y H R. B C H A G; B P, B W O A I L. M E E T K T U O T S T T B O P. - Ephesians 4:1-3

F L O G A N F, B V I W T M A. - Proverbs 11:14

T G A M D O A N, B T I T N O T F A O T S A O T H S, A T T T O E I H C Y. A S I A W Y A, T T V E O T A." - Mathew 28:19-20

The Lost

For God did not send his Son into the world to condemn the world, but to save the world through him.
John 3:17

The Sick, Weary & Discouraged

God is our refuge and strength, an ever-present help in trouble. Therefore we will not fear, though the earth give way and the mountains fall into the heart of the sea, though its waters roar and foam and the mountains quake with their surging.
Psalm 46:1-3

The Oppressed & Enslaved

This is what the Lord Almighty said: "Administer true justice; show mercy and compassion to one another. Do not oppress the widow or the fatherless, the foreigner or the poor. Do not plot evil against each other.'"
Zechariah 7:9-10

F G D N S H S I T W T C T W, B T S T W T H. - John 3:17

G I O R A S, A E H I T. T W W N F, T T E G W A T M F I T H O T S, T I W R A F A T M Q W T S. - Psalm 46:1-3

T I W T L A S: "A T J; S M A C T O A. D N O T W O T F, T F O T P. D N P E A E O." - Zechariah 7:9-10

Wisdom

My goal is that they may be encouraged in heart and united in love, so that they may have the full riches of complete understanding, in order that they may know the mystery of God, namely, Christ, in whom are hidden all the treasures of wisdom and knowledge.
Colossians 2:2-3

Daily Walk

So whether you eat or drink or whatever you do, do it all for the glory of God.
1 Corinthians 10:31

Gratitude & Joy

Therefore, since we are receiving a kingdom that cannot be shaken, let us be thankful, and so worship God acceptably with reverence and awe, for our "God is a consuming fire."
Hebrews 12:28-29

MGITTMBEIHAUIL, STTMHTFROCU, IOTTM KTMOG, N, C, IWAHATTOWAK. - Colossians 2:2-3

SWYEODOWYD, DIAFTGOG. - 1 Corinthians 10:31

T, SWARAKTCBS, LUBT, ASWGAWRAA, FO "GIACF." - Hebrews 12:28-29

Adoration

It is good to praise the Lord and make music to your name, O Most High, proclaiming your love in the morning and your faithfulness at night…
Psalm 92:1-2

Confession

Therefore confess your sins to each other and pray for each other so that you may be healed. The prayer of a righteous person is powerful and effective.
James 5:16

Thanksgiving

So then, just as you received Christ Jesus as Lord, continue to live your lives in him, rooted and built up in him, strengthened in the faith as you were taught, and overflowing with thankfulness.
Colossians 2:6-7

I I G T P T L A M M T Y N, O M H, P Y L I T M A Y F A N... - Psalm 92:1-2

T C Y S T E O A P F E O S T Y M B H. T P O A R P I P A E. - James 5:16

S T, J A Y R C J A L, C T L Y L I H, R A B U I H, S I T F A Y W T, A O W T. - Colossians 2:6-7

Children

But grow in the grace and knowledge
of our Lord and Savior Jesus Christ.
To him be glory both now
and forever! Amen.
2 Peter 3:18

Marriages

Submit to one another out of
reverence for Christ.
Ephesians 5:21

Finances & Stewardship

I know what it is to be in need, and I know
what it is to have plenty. I have learned
the secret of being content in any and
every situation, whether well fed or
hungry, whether living in plenty or in
want. I can do all this through him
who gives me strength.
Philippians 4:12-13

B G I T G A K O O L A S J C. T H B G B N A F! A. - 2 Peter 3:18

S T O A O O R F C. - Ephesians 5:21

I K W I I T B I N, A I K W I I T H P. I H L T S O B C I A A E S, W W F O H,
W L I P O I W. I C D A T T H W G M S. - PHILIPPIANS 4:12-13

The Church

As a prisoner for the Lord, then, I urge you to live a life worthy of the calling you have received. Be completely humble and gentle; be patient, bearing with one another in love. Make every effort to keep the unity of the Spirit through the bond of peace.
Ephesians 4:1-3

Nations & Leaders

For lack of guidance a nation falls, but victory is won through many advisers.
Proverbs 11:14

Missionaries

Therefore go and make disciples of all nations, baptizing them in the name of the Father and of the Son and of the Holy Spirit, and teaching them to obey everything I have commanded you. And surely I am with you always, to the very end of the age."
Matthew 28:19-20

A A P F T L, T, I U Y T L A L W O T C Y H R. B C H A G; B P, B W O A I L.
M E E T K T U O T S T T B O P. - Ephesians 4:1-3

F L O G A N F, B V I W T M A. - Proverbs 11:14

T G A M D O A N, B T I T N O T F A O T S A O T H S, A T T
T O E I H C Y. A S I A W Y A, T T V E O T A." - Mathew 28:19-20

The Lost

For God did not send his Son into the world to condemn the world, but to save the world through him.
John 3:17

The Sick, Weary & Discouraged

God is our refuge and strength, an ever-present help in trouble. Therefore we will not fear, though the earth give way and the mountains fall into the heart of the sea, though its waters roar and foam and the mountains quake with their surging.
Psalm 46:1-3

The Oppressed & Enslaved

This is what the Lord Almighty said: "Administer true justice; show mercy and compassion to one another. Do not oppress the widow or the fatherless, the foreigner or the poor. Do not plot evil against each other.'"
Zechariah 7:9-10

F G D N S H S I T W T C T W, B T S T W T H. - John 3:17

G I O R A S, A E H I T. T W W N F, T T E G W A T M F I T H O T S, T I W R A F A T M Q W T S. - Psalm 46:1-3

T I W T L A S: "A T J; S M A C T O A. D N O T W O T F, T F O T P. D N P E A E O." - Zechariah 7:9-10

Wisdom

My goal is that they may be encouraged in heart and united in love, so that they may have the full riches of complete understanding, in order that they may know the mystery of God, namely, Christ, in whom are hidden all the treasures of wisdom and knowledge.
Colossians 2:2-3

Daily Walk

So whether you eat or drink or whatever you do, do it all for the glory of God.
1 Corinthians 10:31

Gratitude & Joy

Therefore, since we are receiving a kingdom that cannot be shaken, let us be thankful, and so worship God acceptably with reverence and awe, for our "God is a consuming fire."
Hebrews 12:28-29

MGITTMBEIHAUIL, STTMHTFROCU, IOTTM KTMOG, N, C, IWAHATTOWAK. - Colossians 2:2-3

SWYEODOWYD, DIAFTGOG. - 1 Corinthians 10:31

T, SWARAKTCBS, LUBT, ASWGAWRAA, FO "GIACF." - Hebrews 12:28-29

Adoration

He says, "Be still, and know that I am God;
I will be exalted among the nations,
I will be exalted in the earth."
Psalm 46:10

Confession

If we confess our sins, he is faithful and just and
will forgive us our sins and purify us from all
unrighteousness.
1 John 1: 9

Thanksgiving

Give thanks to the Lord, for he is good;
his love endures forever.
1 Chronicles 16:34

H S, "B S, A K T I A G; I W B E A T N, I W B E I T E." - Psalm 46:10

I W C O S, H I F A J A W F U O S A P U F A U. - 1 John 1:9

G T T T L, F H I G; H L E F. - 1 Chronicles 16:34

Children

And Jesus grew in wisdom and stature,
and in favor with God and man.
Luke 2:52

Marriages

By wisdom a house is built,
and through understanding it is established;
Through knowledge its rooms are filled
with rare and beautiful treasures.
Proverbs 24:3-4

Finances & Stewardship

And my God will meet all your needs
according to the riches of his glory
in Christ Jesus.
Philippians 4:19

A J G I W A S, A I F W G A M. - Luke 2:52

B W A H I B, A T U I I E; T K I R A F W R A B T. - Proverbs 24:3-4

A M G W M A Y N A T T R O H G I C J. - Philippians 4:19

The Church

Be devoted to one another in love. Honor one another above yourselves. Never be lacking in zeal, but keep your spiritual fervor, serving the Lord. Be joyful in hope, patient in affliction, faithful in prayer. Share with the Lord's people who are in need. Practice hospitality.
Romans 12: 10-13

Nations & Leaders

Let everyone be subject to the governing authorities, for there is no authority except that which God has established. The authorities that exist have been established by God.
Romans 13:1

Missionaries

As for other matters, brothers and sisters, pray for us that the message of the Lord may spread rapidly and be honored, just as it was with you.
2 Thessalonians 3:1

B D T O A I L. H O A A Y. N B L I Z, B K Y S F, S T L. B J I H, P I A, F I P. S W T L P W A I N. P H. - Romans 12:10-13

L E B S T T G A, F T I N A E T W G H E. T A T E H B E B G. - Romans 13:1

A F O M, B A S, P F U T T M O T L M S R A B H, J A I W W Y. - 2 Thessalonians 3:1

The Lost

For the Son of Man came to seek
and to save the lost.
Luke 19:10

The Sick, Weary & Discouraged

The Lord is close to the brokenhearted
and saves those who are crushed in spirit.
Psalm 34:18

The Oppressed & Enslaved

The Lord is a refuge for the oppressed, a
stronghold in times of trouble. Those who
know your name trust in you, for you, Lord,
have never forsaken those who seek you.
Psalm 7:9-10

F T S O M C T S A T S T L. - Luke 19:10

T L I C T T B A S T W A C I S. - Psalm 34:18

T L I A R F T O, A S I T O T. T W K Y N T I Y, F Y, L, H N F T W S Y. - Psalm 7:9-10

Wisdom

If any of you lacks wisdom, you should ask God, who gives generously to all without finding fault, and it will be given to you.
James 1:5

Daily Walk

Therefore, I urge you, brothers and sisters, in view of God's mercy, to offer your bodies as a living sacrifice, holy and pleasing to God - this is your true and proper worship. Do not conform to the pattern of this world, but be transformed by the renewing of your mind. Then you will be able to test and approve what God's will is - his good, pleasing andperfect will.
Romans 12:1-2

Gratitude & Joy

Rejoice always, pray continually, give thanks in all circumstances; for this is God's will for you in Christ Jesus.
1 Thessalonians 5:16-18

I A O Y L W, Y S A G, W G G T A W F F, A I W B G T Y. - James 1:5

T, I R Y, B A S, I V O G M, T O Y B A A L S, H A P T G - T I Y T A P W. D N C T T P O T W, B B T B T R O Y M. T Y W B A T T A A W G W I - H G, P A P W. - Romans 12:1-2

R A, P C, G T I A C; F T I G W F Y I C J. - 1 Thessalonians 5:16-18

Adoration

The heavens declare the glory of God; the skies proclaim the work of his hands. Day after day they pour forth speech; night after night they reveal knowledge.
Psalm 19:1-2

Confession

...for all have sinned and fall short of the glory of God, and all are justified freely by his grace through the redemption that came by Christ Jesus.
Romans 3:23-24

Thanksgiving

I will give thanks to you, Lord, with all my heart; I will tell of all your wonderful deeds. I will be glad and rejoice in you; I will sing the praises of your name, O Most High.
Psalm 9:1-2

T H D T G O G, T S P T W O H H. D A D T P F S; N A N T R K. - Psalm 19:1-2

F A H S A F S O T G O G, A A A J F B H G T T R T C B C J. - Romans 3:23-24

I W G T T Y, L, W A M H; I W T O A Y W D. I W B G A R I Y; I W S T P O Y N, O M H. - Psalm 9:1-2

Children

…so that Christ may dwell in your hearts through faith. And I pray that you, being rooted and established in love, may have power, together with all the Lord's holy people, to grasp how wide and long and high and deep is the love of Christ.
Ephesians 3:17-18

Marriages

Above all, love each other deeply, because love covers over a multitude of sins.
1 Peter 4:8

Finances & Stewardship

So do not worry, saying, 'What shall we eat?' or 'What shall we drink?' or 'What shall we wear?' For the pagans run after all these things, and your heavenly Father knows that you need them. But seek first his kingdom and his righteousness, and all these things will be given to you as well.
Matthew 6: 31-33

…S T C M D I Y H T F. A I P T Y, B R A E I L, M H P, T W A T L H P, T G H W A L A H A D I T L O C. - Ephesians 3:17-18

A A, L E O D, B L C O A M O S. - 1 Peter 4:8

S D N W, S, 'W S W E?' or 'W S W D?' or 'W S W W?' F T P R A A T T, A Y H F K T Y N T. B S F H K A H R, A A T T W B G T Y A W. - Matthew 6:31-33

The Church

Bless those who persecute you; bless and do not curse. Rejoice with those who rejoice; mourn with those who mourn. Live in harmony with one another. Do not be proud, but be willing to associate with people of low position. Do not be conceited.
Romans 12:14-16

Nations & Leaders

Show proper respect to everyone, love the family of believers, fear God, honor the emperor.
1 Peter 2:17

Missionaries

Declare his glory among the nations, his marvelous deeds among all peoples.
Psalm 96:3

BTWPY; BADNC. RWTWR; MWTWM. LIHWOA. DNBP, BBWTAWPOLP. DNBC. - Romans 12:14-16

SPRTE, LTFOB, FG, HTE. - 1 Peter 2:17

DHGATN, HMDAAP. - Psalm 96:3

The Lost

The Lord is not slow in keeping his promise, as some understand slowness. Instead he is patient with you, not wanting anyone to perish, but everyone to come to repentance.
2 Peter 3:9

The Sick, Weary & Discouraged

We are hard pressed on every side, but not crushed; perplexed, but not in despair; persecuted, but not abandoned; struck down, but not destroyed.
2 Corinthians 4:8-9

The Oppressed & Enslaved

He defends the cause of the fatherless and the widow, and loves the foreigner residing among you, giving them food and clothing.
Deuteronomy 10:18

TLINSIKHP, ASUS. IHIPWY, NWATP, BETCTR. - 2 Peter 3:9

WAHPOES, BNC; P, BNID; P, BNA; SD, BND. - 2 Corinthians 4:8-9

HDTCOTFATW, ALTFRAY, GTFAC. - Deuteronomy 10:18

Wisdom

But the wisdom that comes from heaven is first of all pure; then peace-loving, considerate, submissive, full of mercy and good fruit, impartial and sincere.
James 3:17

Daily Walk

He answered, "Love the Lord your God with all your heart and with all your soul and with all your strength and with all your mind" and, "Love your neighbor as yourself."
Luke 10:27

Gratitude & Joy

I will give thanks to you, Lord, with all my heart; I will tell of all your wonderful deeds. I will be glad and rejoice in you; I will sing the praises of your name, O Most High.
Psalm 9:1-2

BTWTCFHIFOAP;TP-L,C,S,FOMAGF,IAS. - James 3:17

HA,"LTLYGWALYHAWAYSAWAYSAWAYM"A,"LYNAY." - Luke 10:27

IWGTTY,L,WAMH;IWTOAYWD.IWBGARIY;IWSTPOYN,OMH. - Psalm 9:1-2

Adoration

Because your love is better than life, my lips will glorify you. I will praise you as long as I live, and in your name I will lift up my hands. I will be fully satisfied as with the richest of foods; with singing lips my mouth will praise you.
Psalm 63: 3-5

Confession

Whoever conceals their sins does not prosper, but the one who confesses and renounces them finds mercy.
Proverbs 28:13

Thanksgiving

Rejoice always, pray continually, give thanks in all circumstances; for this is God's will for you in Christ Jesus.
1 Thessalonians 5:16-18

B Y L I B T L, M L W G Y. I W P Y A L A I L, A I Y N I W L U M H. I W
B F S A W T R O F; W S L M M W P Y. - Psalm 63:3-5

W C T S D N P, B T O W C A R T F M. - Proverbs 28:13

R A, P C, G T I A C; F T I G W F Y I C J. - 1 Thessalonians 5:16-18

Children

Trust in the Lord with all your heart
and lean not on your own understanding;
in all your ways submit to him,
and he will make your paths straight.
Proverbs 3:5-6

Marriages

Be kind and compassionate to one
another, forgiving each other,
just as in Christ God forgave you.
Ephesians 4:32

Finances & Stewardship

Do not store up for yourselves treasures on
earth, where moths and vermin destroy,
and where thieves break in and steal.
But store up for yourselves treasures in
heaven, where moths and vermin do
not destroy, and where thieves do not
break in and steal. For where your treasure
is, there your heart will be also.
Matthew 6:19-21

TITLWAYHALNOYOU; IAYWSTH, AHWMYPS. - Proverbs 3:5-6

BKACTOA, FEO, JAICGFY. - Ephesians 4:32

DNSUFYTOE, WMAVD, AWTBIAS. BSUFYTIH,
WMAVDND, AWTDNBIAS. FWYTI, TYHWBA. Matthew 6:19-21

The Church

Devote yourselves to prayer, being watchful
and thankful. And pray for us, too, that
God may open a door for our message, so
that we may proclaim the mystery of
Christ, for which I am in chains.
Colossians 4:2-3

Nations & Leaders

I urge, then, first of all, that petitions, prayers,
intercession and thanksgiving be made for all
people— for kings and all those in authority,
that we may live peaceful and quiet lives
in all godliness and holiness.
1 Timothy 2:1-2

Missionaries

Pray also for me, that whenever I speak,
words may be given me so that I will
fearlessly make known the mystery
of the gospel…
Ephesians 3:19

DYTP, BWAT. APFU, T, TGMOADFOM, STWMPTMOC, FWIAIC. - Colossians 4:2-3

IU, T, FOA, TP, P, IATBMFAP-FKAATIA, TWMLPAQLIAGAH. - 1 Timothy 2:1-2

PAFM, TWIS, WMBGMSTIWFMKTMOTG... - Ephesians 3:19

The Lost

For God so loved the world that he
gave his one and only Son,
that whoever believes in him shall not
perish but have eternal life.
John 3:16

The Sick, Weary
& Discouraged

He heals the brokenhearted and
bandages their wounds.
Psalm 147:3

The Oppressed
& Enslaved

The Lord sets prisoners free, the Lord gives
sight to the blind, the Lord lifts up those
who are bowed down, the Lord loves the
righteous. The Lord watches over the
foreigner and sustains the fatherless and
the widow, but he frustrates the
ways of the wicked.
Psalm 146:7-9

F G S L T W T H G H O A O S, T W B I H S N P B H E L. - John 3:16

H H T B A B T W. - Psalm 147:3

T L S P F, T L G S T T B, T L L U T W A B D, T L L T R.
T L W O T F A S T F A T W, B H F T W O T W. - Psalm 146:7-9

Wisdom

The fear of the Lord is the beginning of knowledge, but fools despise wisdom and instruction.
Proverbs 1:7

Daily Walk

In the same way, let your light shine before others, that they may see your good deeds and glorify your Father in heaven.
Matthew 5:16

Gratitude & Joy

Give thanks to the Lord, for he is good; his love endures forever. Let the redeemed of the Lord tell their story—those he redeemed from the hand of the foe…
Psalm 107:1-2

TFOTLITBOK, BFDWAI. - Proverbs 1:7

ITSW, LYLSBO, TTMSYGDAGYFIH. - Matthew 5:16

GTTTL, FHIG; HLEF. LTROTLTTS - THRFTHOTF… - Psalm 107:1-2

Adoration

It is good to praise the Lord and make
music to your name, O Most High,
proclaiming your love in the morning
and your faithfulness at night…
Psalm 92:1-2

Confession

Therefore confess your sins to each other
and pray for each other so that you may be
healed. The prayer of a righteous person is
powerful and effective.
James 5:16

Thanksgiving

So then, just as you received Christ Jesus
as Lord, continue to live your lives in him,
rooted and built up in him, strengthened
in the faith as you were taught, and
overflowing with thankfulness.
Colossians 2:6-7

IIGTPTLAMMTYN, OMH, PYLITMAYFAN... - Psalm 92:1-2

TCYSTEOAPFEOSTYMBH. TPOARPIPAE. - James 5:16

ST, JAYRCJAL, CTLYLIH, RABUIH, SITFAYWT, AOWT. - Colossians 2:6-7

Children

But grow in the grace and knowledge
of our Lord and Savior Jesus Christ.
To him be glory both now
and forever! Amen.
2 Peter 3:18

Marriages

Submit to one another out of
reverence for Christ.
Ephesians 5:21

Finances & Stewardship

I know what it is to be in need, and I know
what it is to have plenty. I have learned
the secret of being content in any and
every situation, whether well fed or
hungry, whether living in plenty or in
want. I can do all this through him
who gives me strength.
Philippians 4:12-13

B G I T G A K O O L A S J C. T H B G B N A F! A. - 2 Peter 3:18

S T O A O O R F C. - Ephesians 5:21

I K W I I T B I N, A I K W I I T H P. I H L T S O B C I A A E S, W W F O H,
W L I P O I W. I C D A T T H W G M S. - PHILIPPIANS 4:12-13

The Church

As a prisoner for the Lord, then, I urge you
to live a life worthy of the calling you have
received. Be completely humble and gentle;
be patient, bearing with one another in love.
Make every effort to keep the unity of
the Spirit through the bond of peace.
Ephesians 4:1-3

Nations & Leaders

For lack of guidance a nation falls,
but victory is won through
many advisers.
Proverbs 11:14

Missionaries

Therefore go and make disciples of all nations,
baptizing them in the name of the Father
and of the Son and of the Holy Spirit, and
teaching them to obey everything I have
commanded you. And surely I am with
you always, to the very end of the age."
Matthew 28:19-20

A A P F T L, T, I U Y T L A L W O T C Y H R. B C H A G; B P, B W O A I L.
M E E T K T U O T S T T B O P. - Ephesians 4:1-3

F L O G A N F, B V I W T M A. - Proverbs 11:14

T G A M D O A N, B T I T N O T F A O T S A O T H S, A T T
T O E I H C Y. A S I A W Y A, T T V E O T A." - Mathew 28:19-20

The Lost

For God did not send his Son into the world to condemn the world, but to save the world through him.
John 3:17

The Sick, Weary & Discouraged

God is our refuge and strength, an ever-present help in trouble. Therefore we will not fear, though the earth give way and the mountains fall into the heart of the sea, though its waters roar and foam and the mountains quake with their surging.
Psalm 46:1-3

The Oppressed & Enslaved

This is what the Lord Almighty said: "Administer true justice; show mercy and compassion to one another. Do not oppress the widow or the fatherless, the foreigner or the poor. Do not plot evil against each other.'"
Zechariah 7:9-10

F G D N S H S I T W T C T W, B T S T W T H. - John 3:17

G I O R A S, A E H I T. T W W N F, T T E G W A T M F I T H O T S, T I W R A F A T M Q W T S. - Psalm 46:1-3

T I W T L A S: "A T J; S M A C T O A. D N O T W O T F, T F O T P. D N P E A E O." - Zechariah 7:9-10

Wisdom

My goal is that they may be encouraged in heart and united in love, so that they may have the full riches of complete understanding, in order that they may know the mystery of God, namely, Christ, in whom are hidden all the treasures of wisdom and knowledge.
Colossians 2:2-3

Daily Walk

So whether you eat or drink or whatever you do, do it all for the glory of God.
1 Corinthians 10:31

Gratitude & Joy

Therefore, since we are receiving a kingdom that cannot be shaken, let us be thankful, and so worship God acceptably with reverence and awe, for our "God is a consuming fire."
Hebrews 12:28-29

MGITTMBEIHAUIL, STTMHTFROCU, IOTTM KTMOG, N, C, IWAHATTOWAK. - Colossians 2:2-3

SWYEODOWYD, DIAFTGOG. - 1 Corinthians 10:31

T, SWARAKTCBS, LUBT, ASWGAWRAA, FO "GIACF." - Hebrews 12:28-29

Adoration

He says, "Be still, and know that I am God;
I will be exalted among the nations,
I will be exalted in the earth."
Psalm 46:10

Confession

If we confess our sins, he is faithful and just and
will forgive us our sins and purify us from all
unrighteousness.
1 John 1: 9

Thanksgiving

Give thanks to the Lord, for he is good;
his love endures forever.
1 Chronicles 16:34

H S, "B S, A K T I A G; I W B E A T N, I W B E I T E." – Psalm 46:10

I W C O S, H I F A J A W F U O S A P U F A U. – 1 John 1:9

G T T T L, F H I G; H L E F. – 1 Chronicles 16:34

Children

And Jesus grew in wisdom and stature,
and in favor with God and man.
Luke 2:52

Marriages

By wisdom a house is built,
and through understanding it is established;
Through knowledge its rooms are filled
with rare and beautiful treasures.
Proverbs 24:3-4

Finances & Stewardship

And my God will meet all your needs
according to the riches of his glory
in Christ Jesus.
Philippians 4:19

A J G I W A S, A I F W G A M. - Luke 2:52

B W A H I B, A T U I I E; T K I R A F W R A B T. - Proverbs 24:3-4

A M G W M A Y N A T T R O H G I C J. - Philippians 4:19

The Church

Be devoted to one another in love. Honor
one another above yourselves. Never be
lacking in zeal, but keep your spiritual
fervor, serving the Lord. Be joyful in hope,
patient in affliction, faithful in prayer.
Share with the Lord's people who are in need.
Practice hospitality.
Romans 12: 10-13

Nations & Leaders

Let everyone be subject to the governing
authorities, for there is no authority
except that which God has established.
The authorities that exist have been
established by God.
Romans 13:1

Missionaries

As for other matters, brothers and sisters,
pray for us that the message of the Lord
may spread rapidly and be honored, just
as it was with you.
2 Thessalonians 3:1

B D T O A I L. H O A A Y. N B L I Z, B K Y S F, S T L. B J I H, P I A, F I P. S W T L P W A I N. P H. - Romans 12:10-13

L E B S T T G A, F T I N A E T W G H E. T A T E H B E B G. - Romans 13:1

A F O M, B A S, P F U T T M O T L M S R A B H, J A I W W Y. - 2 Thessalonians 3:1

The Lost

For the Son of Man came to seek
and to save the lost.
Luke 19:10

The Sick, Weary
& Discouraged

The Lord is close to the brokenhearted
and saves those who are crushed in spirit.
Psalm 34:18

The Oppressed
& Enslaved

The Lord is a refuge for the oppressed, a
stronghold in times of trouble. Those who
know your name trust in you, for you, Lord,
have never forsaken those who seek you.
Psalm 7:9-10

FTSOMCTSATSTL. - Luke 19:10

TLICTTBASTWACIS. - Psalm 34:18

TLIARFTO, ASITOT. TWKYNTIY, FY, L, HNFTWSY. - Psalm 7:9-10

Wisdom

If any of you lacks wisdom, you should ask God, who gives generously to all without finding fault, and it will be given to you.
James 1:5

Daily Walk

Therefore, I urge you, brothers and sisters, in view of God's mercy, to offer your bodies as a living sacrifice, holy and pleasing to God - this is your true and proper worship. Do not conform to the pattern of this world, but be transformed by the renewing of your mind. Then you will be able to test and approve what God's will is - his good, pleasing andperfect will.
Romans 12:1-2

Gratitude & Joy

Rejoice always, pray continually, give thanks in all circumstances; for this is God's will for you in Christ Jesus.
1 Thessalonians 5:16-18

I A O Y L W, Y S A G, W G G T A W F F, A I W B G T Y. - James 1:5

T, I R Y, B A S, I V O G M, T O Y B A A L S, H A P T G - T I Y T A P W. D N C T T P O T W, B B T B T R O Y M. T Y W B A T T A A W G W I - H G, P A P W. - Romans 12:1-2

R A, P C, G T I A C; F T I G W F Y I C J. - 1 Thessalonians 5:16-18

Adoration

The heavens declare the glory of God; the
skies proclaim the work of his hands.
Day after day they pour forth speech; night
after night they reveal knowledge.
Psalm 19:1-2

Confession

...for all have sinned and fall short of the glory
of God, and all are justified freely by his
grace through the redemption that
came by Christ Jesus.
Romans 3:23-24

Thanksgiving

I will give thanks to you, Lord, with all my
heart; I will tell of all your wonderful deeds.
I will be glad and rejoice in you; I will sing
the praises of your name, O Most High.
Psalm 9:1-2

T H D T G O G, T S P T W O H H. D A D T P F S; N A N T R K. - Psalm 19:1-2

F A H S A F S O T G O G, A A A J F B H G T T R T C B C J. - Romans 3:23-24

I W G T T Y, L, W A M H; I W T O A Y W D. I W B G A R I Y; I W S T P O Y N, O M H. - Psalm 9:1-2

Children

…so that Christ may dwell in your hearts through faith. And I pray that you, being rooted and established in love, may have power, together with all the Lord's holy people, to grasp how wide and long and high and deep is the love of Christ.
Ephesians 3:17-18

Marriages

Above all, love each other deeply, because love covers over a multitude of sins.
1 Peter 4:8

Finances & Stewardship

So do not worry, saying, 'What shall we eat?' or 'What shall we drink?' or 'What shall we wear?' For the pagans run after all these things, and your heavenly Father knows that you need them. But seek first his kingdom and his righteousness, and all these things will be given to you as well.
Matthew 6: 31-33

…S T C M D I Y H T F. A I P T Y, B R A E I L, M H P, T W A T L H P, T G H W A L A HA D I T L O C. - Ephesians 3:17-18

A A, L E O D, B L C O A M O S. - 1 Peter 4:8

S D N W, S, 'W S W E?' or 'W S W D?' or 'W S W W?' F T P R A A T T, A Y H F K T Y NT. B S F H K A H R, A A T T W B G T Y A W. - Matthew 6:31-33

The Church

Bless those who persecute you; bless and
do not curse. Rejoice with those who rejoice;
mourn with those who mourn. Live in
harmony with one another. Do not be proud,
but be willing to associate with people
of low position. Do not be conceited.
Romans 12:14-16

Nations & Leaders

Show proper respect to everyone,
love the family of believers,
fear God, honor the emperor.
1 Peter 2:17

Missionaries

Declare his glory among the nations,
his marvelous deeds among all peoples.
Psalm 96:3

BTWPY; BADNC. RWTWR; MWTWM. LIHWOA.
DNBP, BBWTAWPOLP. DNBC. - Romans 12:14-16

SPRTE, LTFOB, FG, HTE. - 1 Peter 2:17

DHGATN, HMDAAP. - Psalm 96:3

The Lost

The Lord is not slow in keeping his promise, as some understand slowness. Instead he is patient with you, not wanting anyone to perish, but everyone to come to repentance.
2 Peter 3:9

The Sick, Weary & Discouraged

We are hard pressed on every side, but not crushed; perplexed, but not in despair; persecuted, but not abandoned; struck down, but not destroyed.
2 Corinthians 4:8-9

The Oppressed & Enslaved

He defends the cause of the fatherless and the widow, and loves the foreigner residing among you, giving them food and clothing.
Deuteronomy 10:18

T L I N S I K H P, A S U S. I H I P W Y, N W A T P, B E T C T R. - 2 Peter 3:9

W A H P O E S, B N C; P, B N I D; P, B N A; S D, B N D. - 2 Corinthians 4:8-9

H D T C O T F A T W, A L T F R A Y, G T F A C. - Deuteronomy 10:18

Wisdom

But the wisdom that comes from heaven is first of all pure; then peace-loving, considerate, submissive, full of mercy and good fruit, impartial and sincere.
James 3:17

Daily Walk

He answered, "Love the Lord your God with all your heart and with all your soul and with all your strength and with all your mind" and, "Love your neighbor as yourself."
Luke 10:27

Gratitude & Joy

I will give thanks to you, Lord, with all my heart; I will tell of all your wonderful deeds. I will be glad and rejoice in you; I will sing the praises of your name, O Most High.
Psalm 9:1-2

B T W T C F H I F O A P; T P-L, C, S, F O M A G F, I A S. - James 3:17

H A, "L T L Y G W A L Y H A W A Y S A W A Y S A W A Y M" A, "L Y N A Y." - Luke 10:27

I W G T T Y, L, W A M H; I W T O A Y W D. I W B G A R I Y; I W S T P O Y N, O M H. - Psalm 9:1-2

Adoration

Because your love is better than life, my lips will glorify you. I will praise you as long as I live, and in your name I will lift up my hands. I will be fully satisfied as with the richest of foods; with singing lips my mouth will praise you.
Psalm 63: 3-5

Confession

Whoever conceals their sins does not prosper, but the one who confesses and renounces them finds mercy.
Proverbs 28:13

Thanksgiving

Rejoice always, pray continually, give thanks in all circumstances; for this is God's will for you in Christ Jesus.
1 Thessalonians 5:16-18

B Y L I B T L, M L W G Y. I W P Y A L A I L, A I Y N I W L U M H. I W B F S A W T R O F; W S L M M W P Y. - Psalm 63:3-5

W C T S D N P, B T O W C A R T F M. - Proverbs 28:13

R A, P C, G T I A C; F T I G W F Y I C J. - 1 Thessalonians 5:16-18

Children

Trust in the Lord with all your heart
and lean not on your own understanding;
in all your ways submit to him,
and he will make your paths straight.
Proverbs 3:5-6

Marriages

Be kind and compassionate to one
another, forgiving each other,
just as in Christ God forgave you.
Ephesians 4:32

Finances & Stewardship

Do not store up for yourselves treasures on
earth, where moths and vermin destroy,
and where thieves break in and steal.
But store up for yourselves treasures in
heaven, where moths and vermin do
not destroy, and where thieves do not
break in and steal. For where your treasure
is, there your heart will be also.
Matthew 6:19-21

TITLWAYHALNOYOU; IAYWSTH, AHWMYPS. - Proverbs 3:5-6

BKACTOA, FEO, JAICGFY. - Ephesians 4:32

DNSUFYTOE, WMAVD, AWTBIAS. BSUFYTIH,
WMAVDND, AWTDNBIAS. FWYTI, TYHWBA. Matthew 6:19-21

The Church

Devote yourselves to prayer, being watchful and thankful. And pray for us, too, that God may open a door for our message, so that we may proclaim the mystery of Christ, for which I am in chains.
Colossians 4:2-3

Nations & Leaders

I urge, then, first of all, that petitions, prayers, intercession and thanksgiving be made for all people— for kings and all those in authority, that we may live peaceful and quiet lives in all godliness and holiness.
1 Timothy 2:1-2

Missionaries

Pray also for me, that whenever I speak, words may be given me so that I will fearlessly make known the mystery of the gospel…
Ephesians 3:19

D Y T P, B W A T. A P F U, T, T G M O A D F O M, S T W M P T M O C, F W I A I C. - Colossians 4:2-3

I U, T, F O A, T P, P, I A T B M F A P - F K A A T I A, T W M L P A Q L I A G A H. - 1 Timothy 2:1-2

P A F M, T W I S, W M B G M S T I W F M K T M O T G… - Ephesians 3:19

The Lost

For God so loved the world that he gave his one and only Son, that whoever believes in him shall not perish but have eternal life.
John 3:16

The Sick, Weary & Discouraged

He heals the brokenhearted and bandages their wounds.
Psalm 147:3

The Oppressed & Enslaved

The Lord sets prisoners free, the Lord gives sight to the blind, the Lord lifts up those who are bowed down, the Lord loves the righteous. The Lord watches over the foreigner and sustains the fatherless and the widow, but he frustrates the ways of the wicked.
Psalm 146:7-9

FGSLTWTHGHOAOS,TWBIHSNPBHEL. - John 3:16

HHTBABTW. - Psalm 147:3

TLSPF,TLGSTTB,TLLUTWABD,TLLTR.
TLWOTFASTFATW, BHFTWOTW. - Psalm 146:7-9

Wisdom

The fear of the Lord is the beginning of
knowledge, but fools despise
wisdom and instruction.
Proverbs 1:7

Daily Walk

In the same way, let your light shine
before others, that they may
see your good deeds and
glorify your Father in heaven.
Matthew 5:16

Gratitude & Joy

Give thanks to the Lord, for he is good; his
love endures forever. Let the redeemed of
the Lord tell their story—those he
redeemed from the hand of the foe…
Psalm 107:1-2

TFOTLITBOK, BFDWAI. - Proverbs 1:7

ITSW, LYLSBO, TTMSYGDAGYFIH. - Matthew 5:16

GTTTL, FHIG; HLEF. LTROTLTTS - THRFTHOTF... - Psalm 107:1-2

Adoration

It is good to praise the Lord and make
music to your name, O Most High,
proclaiming your love in the morning
and your faithfulness at night...
Psalm 92:1-2

Confession

Therefore confess your sins to each other
and pray for each other so that you may be
healed. The prayer of a righteous person is
powerful and effective.
James 5:16

Thanksgiving

So then, just as you received Christ Jesus
as Lord, continue to live your lives in him,
rooted and built up in him, strengthened
in the faith as you were taught, and
overflowing with thankfulness.
Colossians 2:6-7

IIGTPTLAMMTYN, OMH, PYLITMAYFAN... - Psalm 92:1-2

TCYSTEOAPFEOSTYMBH. TPOARPIPAE. - James 5:16

ST, JAYRCJAL, CTLYLIH, RABUIH, SITFAYWT, AOWT. - Colossians 2:6-7

Children

But grow in the grace and knowledge
of our Lord and Savior Jesus Christ.
To him be glory both now
and forever! Amen.
2 Peter 3:18

Marriages

Submit to one another out of
reverence for Christ.
Ephesians 5:21

Finances & Stewardship

I know what it is to be in need, and I know
what it is to have plenty. I have learned
the secret of being content in any and
every situation, whether well fed or
hungry, whether living in plenty or in
want. I can do all this through him
who gives me strength.
Philippians 4:12-13

B G I T G A K O O L A S J C. T H B G B N A F! A. - 2 Peter 3:18

S T O A O O R F C. - Ephesians 5:21

I K W I I T B I N, A I K W I I T H P. I H L T S O B C I A A E S, W W F O H,
W L I P O I W. I C D A T T H W G M S. - PHILIPPIANS 4:12-13

The Church

As a prisoner for the Lord, then, I urge you to live a life worthy of the calling you have received. Be completely humble and gentle; be patient, bearing with one another in love. Make every effort to keep the unity of the Spirit through the bond of peace.
Ephesians 4:1-3

Nations & Leaders

For lack of guidance a nation falls, but victory is won through many advisers.
Proverbs 11:14

Missionaries

Therefore go and make disciples of all nations, baptizing them in the name of the Father and of the Son and of the Holy Spirit, and teaching them to obey everything I have commanded you. And surely I am with you always, to the very end of the age."
Matthew 28:19-20

A A P F T L, T, I U Y T L A L W O T C Y H R. B C H A G; B P, B W O A I L.
M E E T K T U O T S T T B O P. - Ephesians 4:1-3

F L O G A N F, B V I W T M A. - Proverbs 11:14

T G A M D O A N, B T I T N O T F A O T S A O T H S, A T T
T O E I H C Y. A S I A W Y A, T T V E O T A." - Mathew 28:19-20

The Lost

For God did not send his Son into the world to condemn the world, but to save the world through him.
John 3:17

The Sick, Weary & Discouraged

God is our refuge and strength, an ever-present help in trouble. Therefore we will not fear, though the earth give way and the mountains fall into the heart of the sea, though its waters roar and foam and the mountains quake with their surging.
Psalm 46:1-3

The Oppressed & Enslaved

This is what the Lord Almighty said: "Administer true justice; show mercy and compassion to one another. Do not oppress the widow or the fatherless, the foreigner or the poor. Do not plot evil against each other.'"
Zechariah 7:9-10

F G D N S H S I T W T C T W, B T S T W T H. - John 3:17

G I O R A S, A E H I T. T W W N F, T T E G W A T M F I T H O T S, T I W R A F A T M Q W T S. - Psalm 46:1-3

T I W T L A S: "A T J; S M A C T O A. D N O T W O T F, T F O T P. D N P E A E O." - Zechariah 7:9-10

Wisdom

My goal is that they may be encouraged in heart and united in love, so that they may have the full riches of complete understanding, in order that they may know the mystery of God, namely, Christ, in whom are hidden all the treasures of wisdom and knowledge.
Colossians 2:2-3

Daily Walk

So whether you eat or drink or whatever you do, do it all for the glory of God.
1 Corinthians 10:31

Gratitude & Joy

Therefore, since we are receiving a kingdom that cannot be shaken, let us be thankful, and so worship God acceptably with reverence and awe, for our "God is a consuming fire."
Hebrews 12:28-29

M G I T T M B E I H A U I L, S T T M H T F R O C U, I O T T M
K T M O G, N, C, I W A H A T T O W A K. - Colossians 2:2-3

S W Y E O D O W Y D, D I A F T G O G. - 1 Corinthians 10:31

T, S W A R A K T C B S, L U B T, A S W G A W R A A, F O "G I A C F." - Hebrews 12:28-29

Adoration

He says, "Be still, and know that I am God;
I will be exalted among the nations,
I will be exalted in the earth."
Psalm 46:10

Confession

If we confess our sins, he is faithful and just and
will forgive us our sins and purify us from all
unrighteousness.
1 John 1: 9

Thanksgiving

Give thanks to the Lord, for he is good;
his love endures forever.
1 Chronicles 16:34

HS, "B S, A K T I A G; I W B E A T N, I W B E I T E." - Psalm 46:10

I W C O S, H I F A J A W F U O S A P U F A U. - 1 John 1:9

G T T T L, F H I G; H L E F. - 1 Chronicles 16:34

Children

And Jesus grew in wisdom and stature,
and in favor with God and man.
Luke 2:52

Marriages

By wisdom a house is built,
and through understanding it is established;
Through knowledge its rooms are filled
with rare and beautiful treasures.
Proverbs 24:3-4

Finances & Stewardship

And my God will meet all your needs
according to the riches of his glory
in Christ Jesus.
Philippians 4:19

A J G I W A S, A I F W G A M. - Luke 2:52
B W A H I B, A T U I I E; T K I R A F W R A B T. - Proverbs 24:3-4
A M G W M A Y N A T T R O H G I C J. - Philippians 4:19

The Church

Be devoted to one another in love. Honor
one another above yourselves. Never be
lacking in zeal, but keep your spiritual
fervor, serving the Lord. Be joyful in hope,
patient in affliction, faithful in prayer.
Share with the Lord's people who are in need.
Practice hospitality.
Romans 12: 10-13

Nations &
Leaders

Let everyone be subject to the governing
authorities, for there is no authority
except that which God has established.
The authorities that exist have been
established by God.
Romans 13:1

Missionaries

As for other matters, brothers and sisters,
pray for us that the message of the Lord
may spread rapidly and be honored, just
as it was with you.
2 Thessalonians 3:1

B D T O A I L . H O A A Y . N B L I Z , B K Y S F , S T L . B J I H , P I A , F I P . S W T L P W A I N . P H. - Romans 12:10-13

L E B S T T G A , F T I N A E T W G H E . T A T E H B E B G. - Romans 13:1

A F O M , B A S , P F U T T M O T L M S R A B H , J A I W W Y. - 2 Thessalonians 3:1

The Lost

For the Son of Man came to seek
and to save the lost.
Luke 19:10

The Sick, Weary
& Discouraged

The Lord is close to the brokenhearted
and saves those who are crushed in spirit.
Psalm 34:18

The Oppressed
& Enslaved

The Lord is a refuge for the oppressed, a
stronghold in times of trouble. Those who
know your name trust in you, for you, Lord,
have never forsaken those who seek you.
Psalm 7:9-10

F T S O M C T S A T S T L. - Luke 19:10

T L I C T T B A S T W A C I S. - Psalm 34:18

T L I A R F T O, A S I T O T. T W K Y N T I Y, F Y, L, H N F T W S Y. - Psalm 7:9-10

Wisdom

If any of you lacks wisdom, you should ask God, who gives generously to all without finding fault, and it will be given to you.
James 1:5

Daily Walk

Therefore, I urge you, brothers and sisters, in view of God's mercy, to offer your bodies as a living sacrifice, holy and pleasing to God - this is your true and proper worship. Do not conform to the pattern of this world, but be transformed by the renewing of your mind. Then you will be able to test and approve what God's will is - his good, pleasing and perfect will.
Romans 12:1-2

Gratitude & Joy

Rejoice always, pray continually, give thanks in all circumstances; for this is God's will for you in Christ Jesus.
1 Thessalonians 5:16-18

I A O Y L W, Y S A G, W G G T A W F F, A I W B G T Y. - James 1:5

T, I R Y, B A S, I V O G M, T O Y B A A L S, H A P T G - T I Y T A P W. D N C T T P O T W, B B T B T R O Y M. T Y W B A T T A A W G W I - H G, P A P W. - Romans 12:1-2

R A, P C, G T I A C; F T I G W F Y I C J. - 1 Thessalonians 5:16-18

Adoration

The heavens declare the glory of God; the
skies proclaim the work of his hands.
Day after day they pour forth speech; night
after night they reveal knowledge.
Psalm 19:1-2

Confession

...for all have sinned and fall short of the glory
of God, and all are justified freely by his
grace through the redemption that
came by Christ Jesus.
Romans 3:23-24

Thanksgiving

I will give thanks to you, Lord, with all my
heart; I will tell of all your wonderful deeds.
I will be glad and rejoice in you; I will sing
the praises of your name, O Most High.
Psalm 9:1-2

THDTGOG, TSPTWOHH. DADTPFS; NANTRK. - Psalm 19:1-2

FAHSAFSOTGOG, AAAJFBHGTTRTCBCJ. - Romans 3:23-24

IWGTTY, L, WAMH; IWTOAYWD. IWBGARIY; IWSTPOYN, OMH. - Psalm 9:1-2

Children

…so that Christ may dwell in your hearts through faith. And I pray that you, being rooted and established in love, may have power, together with all the Lord's holy people, to grasp how wide and long and high and deep is the love of Christ.
Ephesians 3:17-18

Marriages

Above all, love each other deeply, because love covers over a multitude of sins.
1 Peter 4:8

Finances & Stewardship

So do not worry, saying, 'What shall we eat?' or 'What shall we drink?' or 'What shall we wear?' For the pagans run after all these things, and your heavenly Father knows that you need them. But seek first his kingdom and his righteousness, and all these things will be given to you as well.
Matthew 6: 31-33

…S T C M D I Y H T F. A I P T Y, B R A E I L, M H P, T W A T L H P, T G H W A L A H A D I T L O C. - Ephesians 3:17-18

A A, L E O D, B L C O A M O S. - 1 Peter 4:8

S D N W, S, 'W S W E?' or 'W S W D?' or 'W S W W?' F T P R A A T T, A Y H F K T Y N T. B S F H K A H R, A A T T W B G T Y A W. - Matthew 6:31-33

The Church

Bless those who persecute you; bless and
do not curse. Rejoice with those who rejoice;
mourn with those who mourn. Live in
harmony with one another. Do not be proud,
but be willing to associate with people
of low position. Do not be conceited.
Romans 12:14-16

Nations & Leaders

Show proper respect to everyone,
love the family of believers,
fear God, honor the emperor.
1 Peter 2:17

Missionaries

Declare his glory among the nations,
his marvelous deeds among all peoples.
Psalm 96:3

BTWPY; BADNC. RWTWR; MWTWM. LIHWOA.
DNBP, BBWTAWPOLP. DNBC. - Romans 12:14-16

SPRTE, LTFOB, FG, HTE. - 1 Peter 2:17

DHGATN, HMDAAP. - Psalm 96:3

The Lost

The Lord is not slow in keeping his promise, as some understand slowness. Instead he is patient with you, not wanting anyone to perish, but everyone to come to repentance.
2 Peter 3:9

The Sick, Weary & Discouraged

We are hard pressed on every side, but not crushed; perplexed, but not in despair; persecuted, but not abandoned; struck down, but not destroyed.
2 Corinthians 4:8-9

The Oppressed & Enslaved

He defends the cause of the fatherless and the widow, and loves the foreigner residing among you, giving them food and clothing.
Deuteronomy 10:18

TLINSIKHP, ASUS. IHIPWY, NWATP, BETCTR. - 2 Peter 3:9

WAHPOES, BNC; P, BNID; P, BNA; SD, BND. - 2 Corinthians 4:8-9

HDTCOTFATW, ALTFRAY, GTFAC. - Deuteronomy 10:18

Wisdom

But the wisdom that comes from heaven is first of all pure; then peace-loving, considerate, submissive, full of mercy and good fruit, impartial and sincere.
James 3:17

Daily Walk

He answered, "Love the Lord your God with all your heart and with all your soul and with all your strength and with all your mind" and, "Love your neighbor as yourself."
Luke 10:27

Gratitude & Joy

I will give thanks to you, Lord, with all my heart; I will tell of all your wonderful deeds. I will be glad and rejoice in you; I will sing the praises of your name, O Most High.
Psalm 9:1-2

B T W T C F H I F O A P; T P-L, C, S, F O M A G F, I A S. - James 3:17

H A, "L T L Y G W A L Y H A W A Y S A W A Y S A W A Y M" A, "L Y N A Y." - Luke 10:27

I W G T T Y, L, W A M H; I W T O A Y W D. I W B G A R I Y; I W S T P O Y N, O M H. - Psalm 9:1-2

Adoration

Because your love is better than life, my lips will glorify you. I will praise you as long as I live, and in your name I will lift up my hands. I will be fully satisfied as with the richest of foods; with singing lips my mouth will praise you.

Psalm 63: 3-5

Confession

Whoever conceals their sins does not prosper, but the one who confesses and renounces them finds mercy.

Proverbs 28:13

Thanksgiving

Rejoice always, pray continually, give thanks in all circumstances; for this is God's will for you in Christ Jesus.

1 Thessalonians 5:16-18

B Y L I B T L, M L W G Y. I W P Y A L A I L, A I Y N I W L U M H. I W
B F S A W T R O F; W S L M M W P Y. - Psalm 63:3-5

W C T S D N P, B T O W C A R T F M. - Proverbs 28:13

R A, P C, G T I A C; F T I G W F Y I C J. - 1 Thessalonians 5:16-18

Children

Trust in the Lord with all your heart
and lean not on your own understanding;
in all your ways submit to him,
and he will make your paths straight.
Proverbs 3:5-6

Marriages

Be kind and compassionate to one
another, forgiving each other,
just as in Christ God forgave you.
Ephesians 4:32

Finances & Stewardship

Do not store up for yourselves treasures on
earth, where moths and vermin destroy,
and where thieves break in and steal.
But store up for yourselves treasures in
heaven, where moths and vermin do
not destroy, and where thieves do not
break in and steal. For where your treasure
is, there your heart will be also.
Matthew 6:19-21

TITLWAYHALNOYOU; IAYWSTH, AHWMYPS. - Proverbs 3:5-6

BKACTOA, FEO, JAICGFY. - Ephesians 4:32

DNSUFYTOE, WMAVD, AWTBIAS. BSUFYTIH,
WMAVDND, AWTDNBIAS. FWYTI, TYHWBA. Matthew 6:19-21

The Church

Devote yourselves to prayer, being watchful and thankful. And pray for us, too, that God may open a door for our message, so that we may proclaim the mystery of Christ, for which I am in chains.
Colossians 4:2-3

Nations & Leaders

I urge, then, first of all, that petitions, prayers, intercession and thanksgiving be made for all people— for kings and all those in authority, that we may live peaceful and quiet lives in all godliness and holiness.
1 Timothy 2:1-2

Missionaries

Pray also for me, that whenever I speak, words may be given me so that I will fearlessly make known the mystery of the gospel…
Ephesians 3:19

D Y T P, B W A T. A P F U, T, T G M O A D F O M, S T W M P T M O C, F W I A I C. - Colossians 4:2-3

I U, T, F O A, T P, P, I A T B M F A P - F K A A T I A, T W M L P A Q L I A G A H. - 1 Timothy 2:1-2

P A F M, T W I S, W M B G M S T I W F M K T M O T G… - Ephesians 3:19

The Lost

For God so loved the world that he gave his one and only Son, that whoever believes in him shall not perish but have eternal life.
John 3:16

The Sick, Weary & Discouraged

He heals the brokenhearted and bandages their wounds.
Psalm 147:3

The Oppressed & Enslaved

The Lord sets prisoners free, the Lord gives sight to the blind, the Lord lifts up those who are bowed down, the Lord loves the righteous. The Lord watches over the foreigner and sustains the fatherless and the widow, but he frustrates the ways of the wicked.
Psalm 146:7-9

F G S L T W T H G H O A O S, T W B I H S N P B H E L. - John 3:16

H H T B A B T W. - Psalm 147:3

T L S P F, T L G S T T B, T L L U T W A B D, T L L T R.
T L W O T F A S T F A T W, B H F T W O T W. - Psalm 146:7-9

Wisdom

The fear of the Lord is the beginning of
knowledge, but fools despise
wisdom and instruction.
Proverbs 1:7

Daily Walk

In the same way, let your light shine
before others, that they may
see your good deeds and
glorify your Father in heaven.
Matthew 5:16

Gratitude & Joy

Give thanks to the Lord, for he is good; his
love endures forever. Let the redeemed of
the Lord tell their story—those he
redeemed from the hand of the foe…
Psalm 107:1-2

TFOTLITBOK, BFDWAI. - Proverbs 1:7

ITSW, LYLSBO, TTMSYGDAGYFIH. - Matthew 5:16

GTTTL, FHIG; HLEF. LTROTLTTS - THRFTHOTF… - Psalm 107:1-2

Adoration

It is good to praise the Lord and make
music to your name, O Most High,
proclaiming your love in the morning
and your faithfulness at night…
Psalm 92:1-2

Confession

Therefore confess your sins to each other
and pray for each other so that you may be
healed. The prayer of a righteous person is
powerful and effective.
James 5:16

Thanksgiving

So then, just as you received Christ Jesus
as Lord, continue to live your lives in him,
rooted and built up in him, strengthened
in the faith as you were taught, and
overflowing with thankfulness.
Colossians 2:6-7

IIGTPTLAMMTYN, OMH, PYLITMAYFAN... - Psalm 92:1-2
TCYSTEOAPFEOSTYMBH. TPOARPIPAE. - James 5:16
ST, JAYRCJAL, CTLYLIH, RABUIH, SITFAYWT, AOWT. - Colossians 2:6-7

Children

But grow in the grace and knowledge
of our Lord and Savior Jesus Christ.
To him be glory both now
and forever! Amen.
2 Peter 3:18

Marriages

Submit to one another out of
reverence for Christ.
Ephesians 5:21

Finances & Stewardship

I know what it is to be in need, and I know
what it is to have plenty. I have learned
the secret of being content in any and
every situation, whether well fed or
hungry, whether living in plenty or in
want. I can do all this through him
who gives me strength.
Philippians 4:12-13

B G I T G A K O O L A S J C. T H B G B N A F! A. - 2 Peter 3:18

S T O A O O R F C. - Ephesians 5:21

I K W I I T B I N, A I K W I I T H P. I H L T S O B C I A A E S, W W F O H,
W L I P O I W. I C D A T T H W G M S. - PHILIPPIANS 4:12-13

The Church

As a prisoner for the Lord, then, I urge you to live a life worthy of the calling you have received. Be completely humble and gentle; be patient, bearing with one another in love. Make every effort to keep the unity of the Spirit through the bond of peace.
Ephesians 4:1-3

Nations & Leaders

For lack of guidance a nation falls, but victory is won through many advisers.
Proverbs 11:14

Missionaries

Therefore go and make disciples of all nations, baptizing them in the name of the Father and of the Son and of the Holy Spirit, and teaching them to obey everything I have commanded you. And surely I am with you always, to the very end of the age."
Matthew 28:19-20

A A P F T L, T, I U Y T L A L W O T C Y H R. B C H A G; B P, B W O A I L.
M E E T K T U O T S T T B O P. - Ephesians 4:1-3

F L O G A N F, B V I W T M A. - Proverbs 11:14

T G A M D O A N, B T I T N O T F A O T S A O T H S, A T T
T O E I H C Y. A S I A W Y A, T T V E O T A." - Mathew 28:19-20

The Lost

For God did not send his Son into the world to condemn the world, but to save the world through him.
John 3:17

The Sick, Weary & Discouraged

God is our refuge and strength, an ever-present help in trouble. Therefore we will not fear, though the earth give way and the mountains fall into the heart of the sea, though its waters roar and foam and the mountains quake with their surging.
Psalm 46:1-3

The Oppressed & Enslaved

This is what the Lord Almighty said: "Administer true justice; show mercy and compassion to one another. Do not oppress the widow or the fatherless, the foreigner or the poor. Do not plot evil against each other."
Zechariah 7:9-10

F G D N S H S I T W T C T W, B T S T W T H. - John 3:17

G I O R A S, A E H I T. T W W N F, T T E G W A T M F I T H O T S, T I W R A F A T M Q W T S. - Psalm 46:1-3

T I W T L A S: "A T J; S M A C T O A. D N O T W O T F, T F O T P. D N P E A E O." - Zechariah 7:9-10

Wisdom

My goal is that they may be encouraged in heart and united in love, so that they may have the full riches of complete understanding, in order that they may know the mystery of God, namely, Christ, in whom are hidden all the treasures of wisdom and knowledge.
Colossians 2:2-3

Daily Walk

So whether you eat or drink or whatever you do, do it all for the glory of God.
1 Corinthians 10:31

Gratitude & Joy

Therefore, since we are receiving a kingdom that cannot be shaken, let us be thankful, and so worship God acceptably with reverence and awe, for our "God is a consuming fire."
Hebrews 12:28-29

M G I T T M B E I H A U I L, S T T M H T F R O C U, I O T T M
K T M O G, N, C, I W A H A T T O W A K. - Colossians 2:2-3

S W Y E O D O W Y D, D I A F T G O G. - 1 Corinthians 10:31

T, S W A R A K T C B S, L U B T, A S W G A W R A A, F O "G I A C F." - Hebrews 12:28-29

Adoration

He says, "Be still, and know that I am God;
I will be exalted among the nations,
I will be exalted in the earth."
Psalm 46:10

Confession

If we confess our sins, he is faithful and just and
will forgive us our sins and purify us from all
unrighteousness.
1 John 1:9

Thanksgiving

Give thanks to the Lord, for he is good;
his love endures forever.
1 Chronicles 16:34

H S, "B S, A K T I A G; I W B E A T N, I W B E I T E." – Psalm 46:10

I W C O S, H I F A J A W F U O S A P U F A U. – 1 John 1:9

G T T T L, F H I G; H L E F. – 1 Chronicles 16:34

Children

And Jesus grew in wisdom and stature,
and in favor with God and man.
Luke 2:52

Marriages

By wisdom a house is built,
and through understanding it is established;
Through knowledge its rooms are filled
with rare and beautiful treasures.
Proverbs 24:3-4

Finances & Stewardship

And my God will meet all your needs
according to the riches of his glory
in Christ Jesus.
Philippians 4:19

A J G I W A S, A I F W G A M. - Luke 2:52
B W A H I B, A T U I I E; T K I R A F W R A B T. - Proverbs 24:3-4
A M G W M A Y N A T T R O H G I C J. - Philippians 4:19

The Church

Be devoted to one another in love. Honor one another above yourselves. Never be lacking in zeal, but keep your spiritual fervor, serving the Lord. Be joyful in hope, patient in affliction, faithful in prayer. Share with the Lord's people who are in need. Practice hospitality.
Romans 12: 10-13

Nations & Leaders

Let everyone be subject to the governing authorities, for there is no authority except that which God has established. The authorities that exist have been established by God.
Romans 13:1

Missionaries

As for other matters, brothers and sisters, pray for us that the message of the Lord may spread rapidly and be honored, just as it was with you.
2 Thessalonians 3:1

B D T O A I L. H O A A Y. N B L I Z, B K Y S F, S T L. B J I H, P I A, F I P. S W T L P W A I N. P H. - Romans 12:10-13

L E B S T T G A, F T I N A E T W G H E. T A T E H B E B G. - Romans 13:1

A F O M, B A S, P F U T T M O T L M S R A B H, J A I W W Y. - 2 Thessalonians 3:1

The Lost

For the Son of Man came to seek
and to save the lost.
Luke 19:10

The Sick, Weary & Discouraged

The Lord is close to the brokenhearted
and saves those who are crushed in spirit.
Psalm 34:18

The Oppressed & Enslaved

The Lord is a refuge for the oppressed, a
stronghold in times of trouble. Those who
know your name trust in you, for you, Lord,
have never forsaken those who seek you.
Psalm 7:9-10

FTSOMCTSATSTL. - Luke 19:10

TLICTTBASTWACIS. - Psalm 34:18

TLIARFTO, ASITOT. TWKYNTIY, FY, L, HNFTWSY. - Psalm 7:9-10

Wisdom

If any of you lacks wisdom, you should ask God, who gives generously to all without finding fault, and it will be given to you.
James 1:5

Daily Walk

Therefore, I urge you, brothers and sisters, in view of God's mercy, to offer your bodies as a living sacrifice, holy and pleasing to God - this is your true and proper worship. Do not conform to the pattern of this world, but be transformed by the renewing of your mind. Then you will be able to test and approve what God's will is - his good, pleasing andperfect will.
Romans 12:1-2

Gratitude & Joy

Rejoice always, pray continually, give thanks in all circumstances; for this is God's will for you in Christ Jesus.
1 Thessalonians 5:16-18

I A O Y L W, Y S A G, W G G T A W F F, A I W B G T Y. - James 1:5

T, I R Y, B A S, I V O G M, T O Y B A A L S, H A P T G - T I Y T A P W. D N C T T P O T W, B B T B T R O Y M. T Y W B A T T A A W G W I - H G, P A P W. - Romans 12:1-2

R A, P C, G T I A C; F T I G W F Y I C J. - 1 Thessalonians 5:16-18

Adoration

The heavens declare the glory of God; the skies proclaim the work of his hands. Day after day they pour forth speech; night after night they reveal knowledge.
Psalm 19:1-2

Confession

…for all have sinned and fall short of the glory of God, and all are justified freely by his grace through the redemption that came by Christ Jesus.
Romans 3:23-24

Thanksgiving

I will give thanks to you, Lord, with all my heart; I will tell of all your wonderful deeds. I will be glad and rejoice in you; I will sing the praises of your name, O Most High.
Psalm 9:1-2

THDTGOG, TSPTWOHH. DADTPFS; NANTRK. - Psalm 19:1-2

FAHSAFSOTGOG, AAAJFBHGTTRTCBCJ. - Romans 3:23-24

IWGTTY, L, WAMH; IWTOAYWD. IWBGARIY; IWSTPOYN, OMH. - Psalm 9:1-2

Children

…so that Christ may dwell in your hearts through faith. And I pray that you, being rooted and established in love, may have power, together with all the Lord's holy people, to grasp how wide and long and high and deep is the love of Christ.
Ephesians 3:17-18

Marriages

Above all, love each other deeply, because love covers over a multitude of sins.
1 Peter 4:8

Finances & Stewardship

So do not worry, saying, 'What shall we eat?' or 'What shall we drink?' or 'What shall we wear?' For the pagans run after all these things, and your heavenly Father knows that you need them. But seek first his kingdom and his righteousness, and all these things will be given to you as well.
Matthew 6: 31-33

…S T C M D I Y H T F. A I P T Y, B R A E I L, M H P, T W A T L H P,
T G H W A L A HA D I T L O C. - Ephesians 3:17-18

A A, L E O D, B L C O A M O S. - 1 Peter 4:8

S D N W, S, 'W S W E?' or 'W S W D?' or 'W S W W?' F T P R A A T T, A Y H F K T Y
N T. B S F H K A H R, A A T T W B G T Y A W. - Matthew 6:31-33

The Church

Bless those who persecute you; bless and
do not curse. Rejoice with those who rejoice;
mourn with those who mourn. Live in
harmony with one another. Do not be proud,
but be willing to associate with people
of low position. Do not be conceited.
Romans 12:14-16

Nations & Leaders

Show proper respect to everyone,
love the family of believers,
fear God, honor the emperor.
1 Peter 2:17

Missionaries

Declare his glory among the nations,
his marvelous deeds among all peoples.
Psalm 96:3

BTWPY; BADNC. RWTWR; MWTWM. LIHWOA.
DNBP, BBWTAWPOLP. DNBC. - Romans 12:14-16

SPRTE, LTFOB, FG, HTE. - 1 Peter 2:17

DHGATN, HMDAAP. - Psalm 96:3

The Lost

The Lord is not slow in keeping his promise, as some understand slowness. Instead he is patient with you, not wanting anyone to perish, but everyone to come to repentance.
2 Peter 3:9

The Sick, Weary & Discouraged

We are hard pressed on every side, but not crushed; perplexed, but not in despair; persecuted, but not abandoned; struck down, but not destroyed.
2 Corinthians 4:8-9

The Oppressed & Enslaved

He defends the cause of the fatherless and the widow, and loves the foreigner residing among you, giving them food and clothing.
Deuteronomy 10:18

TLINSIKHP, ASUS. IHIPWY, NWATP, BETCTR. - 2 Peter 3:9

WAHPOES, BNC; P, BNID; P, BNA; SD, BND. - 2 Corinthians 4:8-9

HDTCOTFATW, ALTFRAY, GTFAC. - Deuteronomy 10:18

Wisdom

But the wisdom that comes from heaven is first of all pure; then peace-loving, considerate, submissive, full of mercy and good fruit, impartial and sincere.
James 3:17

Daily Walk

He answered, "Love the Lord your God with all your heart and with all your soul and with all your strength and with all your mind" and, "Love your neighbor as yourself."
Luke 10:27

Gratitude & Joy

I will give thanks to you, Lord, with all my heart; I will tell of all your wonderful deeds. I will be glad and rejoice in you; I will sing the praises of your name, O Most High.
Psalm 9:1-2

B T W T C F H I F O A P; T P-L, C, S, F O M A G F, I A S. - James 3:17

H A, "L T L Y G W A L Y H A W A Y S A W A Y S A W A Y M" A, "L Y N A Y." - Luke 10:27

I W G T T Y, L, W A M H; I W T O A Y W D. I W B G A R I Y; I W S T P O Y N, O M H. - Psalm 9:1-2

Adoration

Because your love is better than life, my lips will glorify you. I will praise you as long as I live, and in your name I will lift up my hands. I will be fully satisfied as with the richest of foods; with singing lips my mouth will praise you.
Psalm 63: 3-5

Confession

Whoever conceals their sins does not prosper, but the one who confesses and renounces them finds mercy.
Proverbs 28:13

Thanksgiving

Rejoice always, pray continually, give thanks in all circumstances; for this is God's will for you in Christ Jesus.
1 Thessalonians 5:16-18

B Y L I B T L, M L W G Y. I W P Y A L A I L, A I Y N I W L U M H. I W
B F S A W T R O F; W S L M M W P Y. - Psalm 63:3-5

W C T S D N P, B T O W C A R T F M. - Proverbs 28:13

R A, P C, G T I A C; F T I G W F Y I C J. - 1 Thessalonians 5:16-18

Children

Trust in the Lord with all your heart
and lean not on your own understanding;
in all your ways submit to him,
and he will make your paths straight.
Proverbs 3:5-6

Marriages

Be kind and compassionate to one
another, forgiving each other,
just as in Christ God forgave you.
Ephesians 4:32

Finances & Stewardship

Do not store up for yourselves treasures on
earth, where moths and vermin destroy,
and where thieves break in and steal.
But store up for yourselves treasures in
heaven, where moths and vermin do
not destroy, and where thieves do not
break in and steal. For where your treasure
is, there your heart will be also.
Matthew 6:19-21

TITLWAYHALNOYOU;IAYWSTH, AHWMYPS. - Proverbs 3:5-6

BKACTOA,FEO,JAICGFY. - Ephesians 4:32

DNSUFYTOE,WMAVD,AWTBIAS.BSUFYTIH,
WMAVDND,AWTDNBIAS.FWYTI,TYHWBA. Matthew 6:19-21

The Church

Devote yourselves to prayer, being watchful and thankful. And pray for us, too, that God may open a door for our message, so that we may proclaim the mystery of Christ, for which I am in chains.
Colossians 4:2-3

Nations & Leaders

I urge, then, first of all, that petitions, prayers, intercession and thanksgiving be made for all people— for kings and all those in authority, that we may live peaceful and quiet lives in all godliness and holiness.
1 Timothy 2:1-2

Missionaries

Pray also for me, that whenever I speak, words may be given me so that I will fearlessly make known the mystery of the gospel…
Ephesians 3:19

D Y T P, B W A T. A P F U, T, T G M O A D F O M, S T W M P T M O C, F W I A I C. - Colossians 4:2-3

I U, T, F O A, T P, P, I A T B M F A P - F K A A T I A, T W M L P A Q L I A G A H. - 1 Timothy 2:1-2

P A F M, T W I S, W M B G M S T I W F M K T M O T G… - Ephesians 3:19

The Lost

For God so loved the world that he gave his one and only Son, that whoever believes in him shall not perish but have eternal life.
John 3:16

The Sick, Weary & Discouraged

He heals the brokenhearted and bandages their wounds.
Psalm 147:3

The Oppressed & Enslaved

The Lord sets prisoners free, the Lord gives sight to the blind, the Lord lifts up those who are bowed down, the Lord loves the righteous. The Lord watches over the foreigner and sustains the fatherless and the widow, but he frustrates the ways of the wicked.
Psalm 146:7-9

F G S L T W T H G H O A O S, T W B I H S N P B H E L. - John 3:16

H H T B A B T W. - Psalm 147:3

T L S P F, T L G S T T B, T L L U T W A B D, T L L T R.
T L W O T F A S T F A T W, B H F T W O T W. - Psalm 146:7-9

Wisdom

The fear of the Lord is the beginning of knowledge, but fools despise wisdom and instruction.
Proverbs 1:7

Daily Walk

In the same way, let your light shine before others, that they may see your good deeds and glorify your Father in heaven.
Matthew 5:16

Gratitude & Joy

Give thanks to the Lord, for he is good; his love endures forever. Let the redeemed of the Lord tell their story—those he redeemed from the hand of the foe…
Psalm 107:1-2

TFOTLITBOK, BFDWAI. - Proverbs 1:7

ITSW, LYLSBO, TTMSYGDAGYFIH. - Matthew 5:16

GTTTL, FHIG; HLEF. LTROTLTTS - THRFTHOTF... - Psalm 107:1-2

Adoration

It is good to praise the Lord and make music to your name, O Most High, proclaiming your love in the morning and your faithfulness at night...
Psalm 92:1-2

Confession

Therefore confess your sins to each other and pray for each other so that you may be healed. The prayer of a righteous person is powerful and effective.
James 5:16

Thanksgiving

So then, just as you received Christ Jesus as Lord, continue to live your lives in him, rooted and built up in him, strengthened in the faith as you were taught, and overflowing with thankfulness.
Colossians 2:6-7

IIGTPTLAMMTYN, OMH, PYLITMAYFAN... - Psalm 92:1-2

TCYSTEOAPFEOSTYMBH. TPOARPIPAE. - James 5:16

ST, JAYRCJAL, CTLYLIH, RABUIH, SITFAYWT, A OWT. - Colossians 2:6-7

Children

But grow in the grace and knowledge
of our Lord and Savior Jesus Christ.
To him be glory both now
and forever! Amen.
2 Peter 3:18

Marriages

Submit to one another out of
reverence for Christ.
Ephesians 5:21

Finances & Stewardship

I know what it is to be in need, and I know
what it is to have plenty. I have learned
the secret of being content in any and
every situation, whether well fed or
hungry, whether living in plenty or in
want. I can do all this through him
who gives me strength.
Philippians 4:12-13

B G I T G A K O O L A S J C. T H B G B N A F! A. - 2 Peter 3:18

S T O A O O R F C. - Ephesians 5:21

I K W I I T B I N, A I K W I I T H P. I H L T S O B C I A A E S, W W F O H,
W L I P O I W. I C D A T T H W G M S. - PHILIPPIANS 4:12-13

The Church

As a prisoner for the Lord, then, I urge you to live a life worthy of the calling you have received. Be completely humble and gentle; be patient, bearing with one another in love. Make every effort to keep the unity of the Spirit through the bond of peace.
Ephesians 4:1-3

Nations & Leaders

For lack of guidance a nation falls, but victory is won through many advisers.
Proverbs 11:14

Missionaries

Therefore go and make disciples of all nations, baptizing them in the name of the Father and of the Son and of the Holy Spirit, and teaching them to obey everything I have commanded you. And surely I am with you always, to the very end of the age."
Matthew 28:19-20

AAPFTL, T, IUYTLALWOTCYHR. BCHAG; BP, BWOAIL.
MEETKTUOTSTTBOP. - Ephesians 4:1-3

FLOGANF, BVIWTMA. - Proverbs 11:14

TGAMDOAN, BTITNOTFAOTSAOTHS, ATT
TOEIHCY. ASIAWYA, TTVEOTA." - Mathew 28:19-20

The Lost

For God did not send his Son into the world to condemn the world, but to save the world through him.
John 3:17

The Sick, Weary & Discouraged

God is our refuge and strength, an ever-present help in trouble. Therefore we will not fear, though the earth give way and the mountains fall into the heart of the sea, though its waters roar and foam and the mountains quake with their surging.
Psalm 46:1-3

The Oppressed & Enslaved

This is what the Lord Almighty said: "Administer true justice; show mercy and compassion to one another. Do not oppress the widow or the fatherless, the foreigner or the poor. Do not plot evil against each other.'"
Zechariah 7:9-10

F G D N S H S I T W T C T W, B T S T W T H. - John 3:17

G I O R A S, A E H I T. T W W N F, T T E G W A T M F I T H O T S, T I W R A F A T M Q W T S. - Psalm 46:1-3

T I W T L A S: "A T J; S M A C T O A. D N O T W O T F, T F O T P. D N P E A E O." - Zechariah 7:9-10

Wisdom

My goal is that they may be encouraged in heart and united in love, so that they may have the full riches of complete understanding, in order that they may know the mystery of God, namely, Christ, in whom are hidden all the treasures of wisdom and knowledge.
Colossians 2:2-3

Daily Walk

So whether you eat or drink or whatever you do, do it all for the glory of God.
1 Corinthians 10:31

Gratitude & Joy

Therefore, since we are receiving a kingdom that cannot be shaken, let us be thankful, and so worship God acceptably with reverence and awe, for our "God is a consuming fire."
Hebrews 12:28-29

MGITTMBEIHAUIL, STTMHTFROCU, IOTTM KTMOG, N, C, IWAHATTOWAK. - Colossians 2:2-3

SWYEODOWYD, DIAFTGOG. - 1 Corinthians 10:31

T, SWARAKTCBS, LUBT, ASWGAWRAA, FO "GIACF." - Hebrews 12:28-29

76417515R00089

Made in the USA
San Bernardino, CA
11 May 2018